I0211715

The Importance of God's Word

Meditations on Psalm 119

David Anderson, Ian D Britton,
Brian Donaldson, Yannick Ford,
David M Hughes, Jonathan Hughes,
Gordon D Kell, Peter Ollerhead,
David G Pulman, George E Stevens,
Paul Thomson, Stephen Thomson.

Compiled and Edited by David Anderson

Scripture Truth Publications

FIRST EDITION

FIRST PRINTING October 2021

ISBN: 978-0-901860-99-6 (paperback)

© Copyright 2021 Truth for Today/Scripture Truth

A publication of Scripture Truth

Published by Scripture Truth Publications 31-33 Glover Street, Crewe, Cheshire CW1 3LD

Scripture Truth is an imprint of Central Bible Hammond Trust, a charitable trust

Typesetting by John Rice

Foreword

This book is an edited compilation of the transcripts of all the talks broadcast on the *Truth for Today, The Bible Explained* radio programme between September 2017 and March 2020 in the series "Psalm 119 – The importance of God's Word".

As several of the speakers referred to the structure of Psalm 119 during their talk, these comments have been collated, condensed, and incorporated into the Introduction of this book. Originally, the introduction was part of the first talk (on ALEPH, verses 1-8).

David Anderson
Spring, 2021

THE IMPORTANCE OF GOD'S WORD

Contents

Introduction

DAVID ANDERSON & YANNICK FORD

As many people know, Psalm 119 is the longest of the psalms – it has 176 verses! It is also the longest chapter in the Bible. Perhaps for that reason the 176 verses are seldom, or never, read completely – either in public or private meditation. Psalm 119 is divided into 22 stanzas (or sections) of 8 verses each, with each stanza corresponding to one of the 22 letters of the Hebrew alphabet. In some translations the Hebrew letter of the alphabet is printed at the head of each stanza. It is a so-called 'acrostic' psalm (and one of several acrostic poems which occur in the Old Testament). For example, in the original Hebrew text, verses 1-8 of Psalm 119 all start with a Hebrew letter ALEPH (English "a"); and so on. The meaning of these Hebrew letters often plays a role in being the dominant theme of the stanza. This was probably a memory aid, as it is a lot easier to memorise things if you can attach them to a simple structure in your mind. Of course, it's very difficult to reproduce this effect in an English translation!

What is Psalm 119 all about? Really, just one theme – the excellency and value of the Word of God. For Christian believers, the Word of God not only furnishes us with a knowledge of the living God, but it also speaks of the Christ who has revealed Him. In John 1:1-14, Jesus Christ is called "the Word". He is "the Alpha and Omega" (Revelation 1:8, 11; 21:6; 22:13) – the "A-Z"[1] of God.

Psalm 119 is full of verses explaining the benefit of God's Word, expressing the Psalmist's delight in it, his desire to keep it, his asking for help to live according to it, and so on. The great Victorian preacher Charles Spurgeon wrote a commentary on Psalm 119, in which he quoted part of Matthew Henry's account of his father Philip. It read:

> "Once, pressing the study of the Scriptures, he advised us to take a verse of this Psalm every morning to meditate upon, and so go over the Psalm twice in the year; 'and that', saith he, 'will bring you to be in love with all the rest of the Scriptures.' He often said, 'All grace grows as love to the word of God grows.'"[2]

This is very helpful, because it is somewhat difficult to see an overarching structure in Psalm 119; and so it can seem daunting at the first sight. However, looking at one verse a day really helps to increase our love and respect for the Word of God, as Philip Henry said it would.

Spurgeon himself was hesitant when he came to write a commentary on Psalm 119. In his fifth volume of *The Treasury of David*, in the preface he said:

[1] In Hebrew the equivalent would be "the ALEPH and TAU".

[2] Charles Haddon Spurgeon, *The Treasury of David containing an original exposition of the Book of Psalms; a collection of illustrative extracts from the whole range of literature; a series of homiletical hints upon almost every verse, and lists of writers upon each Psalm*, Passmore & Alabaster: London, 1870-86.

"I have been bewildered in the expanse of the One Hundred and Nineteenth Psalm, which makes up the bulk of this volume. Its dimensions and its depth alike overcame me. It spread itself out before me like a vast, rolling prairie, to which I could see no bound, and this alone created a feeling of dismay. Its expanse was unbroken by a bluff or headland, and hence it threatened a monotonous task, although the fear has not been realized."

However he came to appreciate the wonderful blessing of this unique Psalm:

"I have now crossed the great plain for myself, but not without persevering, and, I will add, pleasurable, toil. ...Those who have never studied it may pronounce it commonplace, and complain of its repetitions; but to the thoughtful student it is like the great deep, full, so as never to be measured; and varied, so as never to weary the eye."

Charles Bridges, a great evangelical Christian who was a contemporary of Charles Spurgeon, also wrote a commentary on Psalm 119. In it he said:

"The Writer is free to confess, that his main design in the study of this Psalm was to furnish a correct standard of Evangelical sincerity for the habitual scrutiny of his own heart."[3]

[3] Charles Bridges, *Exposition of Psalm CXIX as illustrative of the Character and Exercises of Christian Experience*, page vi, R.B.Seeley & W.Burnside: London, 1827.

In other words, he was saying that he was principally concerned with listening to the Word of God and seeing what it had to say *to him*, before teaching others. The Word of God is indeed a two-edged sword:

> "The word of God is living and powerful, and sharper than any two-edged sword, piercing even to the division of soul and spirit, and of joints and marrow, and is a discerner of the thoughts and intents of the heart. And there is no creature hidden from His sight, but all things are naked and open to the eyes of Him to whom we must give account" (Hebrews 4:12-13).

When we read and study the Word of God, we need first and foremost to see and understand what it is saying *to us*. Spurgeon also quoted Augustine on how to approach Psalm 119:

> "It seemeth not to need an expositor, but only a reader and a listener."[4]

Not so much an expositor, but just someone who is willing to read it and then listen to what it is saying. Psalm 119 is not a complicated psalm, full of mysteries and difficulties. Instead, it is simple and direct; and it speaks to our hearts and to our consciences. Reading it bit by bit, and meditating on it, as Philip Henry recommended, is a very good way of being "a reader and a listener", as Augustine proposed.

In summary then, Psalm 119 is a lengthy collection of meditations on the Word of God. Let us begin with a few principles and thoughts that will help us understand the

---

[4] Augustine, *Expositions of the Book of Psalms, Volume V, Psalm CII-CXXV*, John Henry Parker: Oxford, 1853, page 313.

psalm. First of all, let us consider all these different words for God's Word that we come across:

1. Law.
2. Testimonies.
3. Precepts.
4. Statutes.
5. Commandments.
6. Judgements.
7. Word.
8. Ordinances.

Some expositors think that these words all have different shades of meaning, and that they bring out one or other particular aspect of the Word of God.[5] Others seem to suggest that they may be synonyms for the Word of God. One would have to do several word studies, looking up each time these specific words are used in the Old Testament to see if there are particular meanings associated with them. It seems likely that the different words were used for a reason. We get some help on these words by looking at Psalm 19, where a good many of these different words are used together with a practical explanation for each of them.

> "The law of the LORD is perfect, converting the soul; the testimony of the LORD is sure, making wise the simple; the statutes of the LORD are right, rejoicing the heart; the commandment of the LORD is pure, enlightening the eyes; the fear of

---

5 For example: Derek Kidner, *Psalms 73-150*, Tyndale Old Testament Commentaries, Inter-Varsity Press, London, 1975, pages 417-419; W. Graham Scroggie, *The Psalms*, Pickering & Inglis Ltd, London, 1967, pages 171-173.

the LORD is clean, enduring forever; the
judgments of the LORD are true and
righteous altogether" (Psalm 19:7-9).

The *law* is spoken of as perfect and converting the soul.
The "law" is in some sense the whole of God's Word,
which shows us what God requires. The word for law,
"torah", can mean "instruction". We know, of course,
that we cannot be converted by *keeping* the law (see
Romans 3:20-22). That is why the Lord Jesus came to be
our Saviour – but it is the *law*, that is, God's Word, that
instructs us and tells us what we need to know.

The *testimony* of the LORD is said to be sure – that means
that what God has witnessed, or testified, about Himself
is reliable. And that means that we can take Him at His
Word. We will never be deceived if we trust in God's
testimony.

The *statutes* of the LORD are said to be right – so what
God commands commends itself to us because it is
righteous. The effect of these statutes is to cause the
godly to rejoice in them. And so we can continue, looking
at these different terms for God's Word and the meanings
attached to them.

The *judgments* of the LORD are true and righteous
altogether. Whatever the situation, however complicated
the issues may be, the final *judgment* of the LORD on the
matter will be found to be both according to truth and to
righteousness.

The following is an analysis of these synonyms found in
the New King James Version, which Gordon Kell
provided as an introduction to his talk on SAMECH.

Throughout the psalm, the Word of God is described mainly in the following words:

"Commandment" appears 21 times. The psalmist uses it to refer to definite commands which require obedience. It teaches that God's Word requires our obedience.

"Judgment" appears 18 times and it relates to judicial decisions. In the Pentateuch it referred to the laws which followed the Ten Commandments. "Judgment" teaches us about the application of God's Word across all the circumstances of life and the confidence we can have in it.

"Law" is used 15 times in the psalm to emphasise the Word of God as instruction for life. It is particularly linked with the law outlined in the Pentateuch. The psalmist upholds God's Word as that which guides him through life. It teaches us about how God's Word guides us spiritually.

"Precepts" occurs 21 times and is used poetically for injunctions. It is only found in the books of Psalms. It teaches about applying God's Word to govern our thoughts, words, and actions.

"Statutes" occurs 21 times always in the plural. Its literal meaning is "things inscribed" referring to laws. Inscribing has a sense of permanence, and it teaches us about the eternal character of God's Word.

"Testimony" appears 21 times in the plural and conveys a declaration of the will of God. It is usually translated "statutes". It teaches us about the standards of conduct God desires to see in His people.

"Way" appears 26 times, and it teaches us about the pattern of life the Word of God outlines for us.

"Word" is used 36 times as a general term for God's revelation. In Deuteronomy 4:13, we read:

> "So, He declared to you His covenant which He commanded you to perform, the Ten Commandments; and He wrote them on two tablets of stone."

"Ten commandments" in Deuteronomy 4:13 has the literal meaning of "ten words." The psalmist uses "word" to describe God's revelation to men. It teaches us that God reveals Himself through His Word.

These words are used extensively throughout the psalm to focus the reader on the Word of God and the blessings which flow from it when we read it, believe it, and obey it. Alongside these eight synonyms, the psalmist also describes:

- his personal delight in God's Word.
- his love for God's Word.
- his obedience to God's Word.
- his meditation of God's Word.
- his joy in God's Word.

The psalmist refers to himself as God's servant twelve times. As such, the psalmist sought God to refresh and preserve him in his service. The psalmist teaches us about God's sustaining power to undertake and fulfil His will in our lives.

In summary, the synonyms the psalmist uses in Psalm 119 teach us that God's Word:

- requires our obedience.
- can be trusted in all the circumstances of life.
- guides us spiritually.

- governs our thoughts, words, and actions.

- is eternal.

- provides standards of conduct.

- provides a pattern for our lives.

- reveals God to us.

We do not know who wrote Psalm 119, because no name is given! Charles Spurgeon thought that it was David. He made an interesting suggestion:

> "The earlier verses are of such a character as to lend themselves to the hypothesis that the author was a young man, while many of the later passages could only have suggested themselves to age and wisdom."

So it is a bit like the psalm being David's spiritual journal through his life. Whether that was so or not, we simply do not know, but it is an interesting idea, and it fits in well with Philip Henry's suggestion of reading and meditating on one verse of this psalm a day. We can make it into a sort of journal for ourselves as we go through the psalm, learning more about God's Word.

Of course, what we do know is that the author was an Old Testament writer. That is important because we live in a different time to the Old Testament saints, now that the Lord Jesus has come, and lived and died, and risen again. In the Old Testament, faithful men and women sought to obey God's law. Keeping the law was what was required. Of course, no-one could do so perfectly, and so God's grace was always necessary. But the point was, God was testing His people under the law.

He knew that they could not keep it, but they needed to learn that for themselves. The Apostle Paul says:

> "Therefore by the deeds of the law no flesh will be justified in His sight, for by the law is the knowledge of sin. But now the righteousness of God apart from the law is revealed, being witnessed by the Law and the Prophets, even the righteousness of God, through faith in Jesus Christ, to all and on all who believe" (Romans 3:20-22).

That is why Jesus came to die for us. Now, we live in the power of His Spirit. He is the One who enables us to keep His requirements (compare Romans 8:1-4).

We live in the day of grace. It is important to remember that when we read the Psalms. On the one hand, we must remember the Old Testament context in which the Psalms were written; and on the other hand, we wear 'New Testament glasses', so to speak, so that we can be blessed and instructed by considering the sentiments of the Psalms in terms of the day of grace in which we live.

א

1. ALEPH – verses 1-8

Yannick Ford

Verses 1-2: "Blessed are the undefiled in the way, who walk in the law of the LORD! Blessed are those who keep His testimonies, who seek Him with the whole heart."

The Psalmist starts by stating the blessedness, or happiness, of those who are "undefiled in the way, who walk in the law of the LORD, who keep His testimonies and who seek Him with a whole heart" (verse 1). Today, in the day of grace, the same principle applies. Consider these verses:

> "Jesus answered and said to him, 'If anyone loves Me, he will keep My word; and My Father will love him, and We will come to him and make Our home with him'" (John 14:23).

> "As the Father loved Me, I also have loved you; abide in My love. If you keep My commandments, you will abide in My

> love, just as I have kept My Father's
> commandments and abide in His love.
> These things I have spoken to you, that
> My joy may remain in you, and that your
> joy may be full" (John 15:9-11).

There is a joy promised by the Lord Jesus to those who keep His words, just as the psalmist spoke about the blessedness of those who walked in the law of the LORD (Psalm 119:1). If we do not keep His ways, if we sin, we know that we can confess this and repent, as John assures us:

> "If we confess our sins, He is faithful and
> just to forgive us our sins and to cleanse
> us from all unrighteousness" (1 John 1:9).

But when we sin, we grieve the Holy Spirit. We do not lose our salvation, but we lose the enjoyment of it and then we do not experience the blessedness that the psalmist speaks of. One secret no doubt is to seek God with the whole heart (Psalm 119:2b). It is a good question for each one of us to ask ourselves: "Am I whole-hearted?"

Verse 3: "They also do no iniquity; they walk in His ways."

Verse 3 says that these blessed people do no iniquity. Of course, no one is perfect. John tells us that:

> "If we say that we have no sin, we deceive
> ourselves, and the truth is not in us"
> (1 John 1:8).

But insofar as we rely on the strength of the Holy Spirit, we can seek to act in our new nature, which does not want to sin:

"Whoever has been born of God does not sin, for His seed remains in him; and he cannot sin, because he has been born of God" (1 John 3:9).

This is very encouraging! We have been given a new nature that *wants* to walk in God's ways, even as Ephesians 4:24 tells us:

"And that you put on the new man which was created according to God, in true righteousness and holiness."

Verses 4-5: "You have commanded us to keep Your precepts diligently. Oh, that my ways were directed to keep Your statutes!"

Verses 4-5 express a standard, and then a longing on the part of the psalmist that he could reach that standard. In the day of the Law, this would no doubt have been the experience of godly men and women – they knew that God expected them to keep His law, but they also knew that they could not do it perfectly.

Paul experienced the same thing in Romans 7:

"For I delight in the law of God according to the inward man. But I see another law in my members, warring against the law of my mind, and bringing me into captivity to the law of sin which is in my members" (7:22-23).

Now we live in a privileged time. Jesus has kept the law, and He has borne all our sins. He is the One who is able! Read Romans 8:1-17, to see how this is clearly explained by the Apostle Paul.

Verse 6: "Then I would not be ashamed, when I look into all Your commandments."

The psalmist is saying that if his ways were really directed to keep God's statutes, then, when he read them, he would not be ashamed, because they would commend him rather than condemn him. What about us? How does this sentiment of the psalmist apply to us, in our day? We also need not be ashamed, if we trust and rely on the Lord Jesus. John exhorts us to abide in Him, so that we will not be ashamed:

> "And now, little children, abide in Him, that when He appears, we may have confidence and not be ashamed before Him at His coming" (1 John 2:28).

Verses 7-8: "I will praise You with uprightness of heart, when I learn Your righteous judgments. I will keep Your statutes; oh, do not forsake me utterly!"

The psalmist expresses such a desire in verses 7-8. Here we need to bring in a wonderful New Testament truth that encourages us. We know that we will never be forsaken, so that we do not need to fear that this might happen. We are told this plainly in Hebrews 13:5:

> "For He Himself has said, 'I will never leave you nor forsake you.'"

Therefore we can seek to learn more and more about God and His Word, knowing that He will always be present for our help and blessing. Like the psalmist, we will praise God more and more as we learn more and more about His Word.

ב

2.   BETH – verses 9-16

David M Hughes

Introduction

Where do you go to for advice about life? How do you decide what you will do and what you will not? On what basis do you make those decisions? For most of us, our values and principles are shaped by a number of sources. Usually parents have a big influence on what we think is important. The society we live in has values that will have an impact on how we think. Friends, extended family, and perhaps even social media, all play a role in shaping the person you are.

But how do you know if your system of values is good or not? Whether you consider yourself a religious person or not, I suspect most people want to live a good life. Most people do not want to waste their life. How can we live a life that is good and fulfilling? What will keep us from ruining our lives and wasting them? The psalmist of Psalm 119 asked exactly these questions, and our meditation is about the answers he gives. He asks and immediately answers:

"How can a young man cleanse his way?
By taking heed according to Your word"
(verse 9).

For the psalmist, God's Word was to be the most important influence on his life. What he learnt in the Scripture was to impact on his life more than the advice of anyone else. For him, any other influences were useful only in so far as they gave advice in line with the teaching of Scripture. It's worth noting that only a small selection of the books of the Old Testament would have been available to the psalmist. For us today, God's will is revealed to us in a fuller and more complete way, through the teaching of the rest of the Old Testament and, most importantly, the New Testament.

The psalmist's advice is just as true for us today. The only way to live a life that is pleasing to God, and not wasted, is to live according to God's Word. Many of your friends and neighbours might scoff at such a statement: "Who would live their lives following the teaching of a dusty old relic?" For them, the Bible is no more than a really old collection of fairy tales and myths. If that is your view of the Bible, could I encourage you to pick it up and read it again? Of course, there are parts that are difficult to understand and seem strange to our twenty-first Century way of thinking, but the Bible declares that God's Word is:

> "Living and powerful, and sharper than any two-edged sword, piercing even to the division of soul and spirit, and of joints and marrow, and is a discerner of the thoughts and intents of the heart" (Hebrews 4:12).

2. BETH – VERSES 9-16

Why not read the Bible and see if it has anything to say about the intents of your heart? You will find, like many millions over the years, that God's Word really is living and powerful and relevant to us today.

As stated in the Introduction to this book, the structure of Psalm 119 would aid its memorisation: a reminder of the importance that Jews in the Old Testament placed on learning the Scriptures by heart. Memorisation is a hard task. It is certainly not easy, and is made harder for us since, unlike them, we have not been taught to memorise by heart from a very young age. However, these verses show the benefits that learning the Scriptures, and hiding them in our hearts, will have on our lives. You do not need to start by memorising huge chunks of Scripture at once. Even learning one verse a month would soon enough give you a treasury of wisdom stored up in your mind. Remember, too I am not encouraging learning parts of the Bible for the sake of completeness. There are no prizes for memorising the whole Bible by heart. What matters is what we do with the verses as the Holy Spirit reminds us of them as we go about our lives. Even just a few verses stored in our minds and meditated on and acted upon as we are involved in our daily business might make a huge difference to our lives.

It is not always possible, or helpful, to split up the Psalms into exact sections for analysis or study. The Psalms were Hebrew poems, and poems or songs do not always have the same exact logical structure that other forms of writing might have. However, it is helpful to notice these general points about the verses 9-16. The stanza starts with a question:

"How can a young man cleanse his way?"
(verse 9).

Verses 10-16 give an expanded answer, in which there are:

1. Four things the psalmist *has done* (verses 10-14).
2. Four things that the psalmist *will do* (verses 15-16).

Living according to God's Word is an ongoing process. Things that the psalmist did in the past were now going to help him live in the present. But equally, his past experiences and actions did not guarantee his current faithfulness. So, in verses 15-16 he makes the four declarations of things he would do. Living a life that is pleasing to God requires continual diligence. Things we do now will affect our ability to live faithfully in the future. If our current actions are like those of verses 10-14, then that will help keep us in the right frame of mind, and in dependence on God, so that in the future we can make the bold declarations of verses 15-16. Thankfully, that does not mean that if our past has been less than ideal, or even if our current actions have not been as faithful to God as we might like, that all hope is lost. The advice in this stanza of Psalm 119 can be put into practice at any point in life; and needs to be put into practice in a fresh way each day.

Verse 9: "How can a young man cleanse his way? By taking heed according to Your word."

Verses 1-8 stated that those who are undefiled in the way, who keep God's testimonies, and seek Him with their whole hearts, are blessed. The question in verse 9 follows on from this and asks, "How can I experience that kind of blessing?" or "How can I live that kind of life?" A good question to ask. Psalm 119:1-8 describe the great blessing of living in the way God says is best. What a good response to want to live that way! All of us should ask ourselves if we are really living according to God's Word. Verses 10-14 give us a picture of what our lives will look like if we live according to God's Word, as the four occurrences of the phrase "I have" show.

Verse 10: "With my whole heart I have sought You; Oh, let me not wander from Your commandments!"

The first way to live according to God's Word, is to seek after Him with our whole hearts. This would have been familiar to the Jewish readers. They would remember that Deuteronomy told them:

> "You shall love the LORD your God with
> all your heart, with all your soul, and with
> all your strength" (Deuteronomy 6:5).[6]

God wants His people to follow Him with a whole heart. He does not want us to be drawn away after other things.

We all feel that there are so many things in life that demand our attention and take up our time. Some things are necessary, like family responsibilities with associated work commitments and financial matters. Many other things may interest us – things like sports, politics, fashion, television and so on. So we, like the psalmist, need to pray:

> "Oh, let me not wander from Your
> commandments" (verse 10b).

The challenge for us is not to let these various "other things", no matter how legitimate, overtake God in our

---

[6] In fact the book of Deuteronomy reminded them to serve the LORD with all their hearts five times in total (Deuteronomy 6:5, 10:12, 11:13, 13:3, 30:6) and Joshua reminds them of it as well (Joshua 22:5).

priorities. God must have the first place in our hearts, and our seeking after Him is to colour every other sphere of our lives. Not that we can have no other interests or responsibilities, but that our actions are all to be influenced by our seeking God with our whole hearts. Seeking after God should make a difference in how I act with my family, or in my job, or in pursuing my other interests.

Verses 11-12: "Your word I have hidden in my heart, that I might not sin against You. Blessed are You, O Lord! Teach me Your statutes."

Someone has said of this verse that it is "the best thing in the best place for the best reason":

- the best thing, God's Word.

- the best place, hidden in our hearts.

- the best reason, that we might not sin against God.

The verse presents us with some challenges. What do we fill our hearts with? As already mentioned, so many things cry out for our attention. It occurred to me recently that I was spending considerable amounts of my leisure time on secular things which interested me, but not always anywhere near as much time reading the Bible and thinking about its content. It is not that having interests outside of the Bible is necessarily wrong and that the only legitimate use of spare time is reading the Bible. But God's Word should certainly have a high importance in a believer's life. What a great privilege we have, here in the United Kingdom, of having the Bible so freely available (and in so many translations) for us to read! What a great blessing to have written down for us everything God wants us to know. For us New Testament believers, we can possess this perfection of knowledge of God in Christ:

> "Filled with the [full] knowledge of his will in all wisdom and spiritual understanding" (Colossians 1:9).

In the end analysis, some knowledge we acquire is of limited value – useful only for our lives now upon earth. Other acquired knowledge is essentially useless, but God's Word is not like that. It abides forever:

> "The word of the LORD endures forever. Now this is the word which by the gospel was preached to you" (1 Peter 1:25).

> "The world is passing away, and the lust of it: but he who does the will of God abides for ever" (1 John 2:17).

May the Lord help all of us to truly value His Word.

A second challenge from our verse is what do we do with God's Word? If you have a Bible, what do you do with it? Does it sit on the shelf gathering dust only to come out at special occasions? Perhaps you read it every week at a church gathering, but by the time you get home you cannot even remember what part of the Bible was read. Maybe you read it every day, but as soon as you leave the door of your house you have forgotten what you read. The psalmist says he hides God's Word in his heart. He values God's Word. He treats it as precious. He lets it sink down into his heart. He retains what he has read. Would that this was our desire! Keep God's Word in your heart! Of course, there will be days where our uptake is better than on others but let us determine as much as we can to let God's Word take root in our hearts. There are many

things that help with this. For example, learning some of
the verses you read, or writing one or more down and
keeping the piece of paper with you to look at and think
about it from time to time during the day. Some keep
notes of what they read. No doubt there are many other
ways to help us retain more of what we read.

What effect does God's Word have in our lives? The
psalmist did not hide God's Word in his heart so that he
could win Bible trivia quizzes or so that he could impress
people with his great knowledge. He did not even
primarily hide God's Word in his heart so that he could
teach other people. First and foremost, he hid God's
Word in his heart so that he would not *sin* against God.
His first concern was to sin less and live a life that pleased
God. Let us keep that in mind as we read the Scriptures.
No matter what other benefits may come from a greater
knowledge of God's Word, firstly it is to transform our
lives to make us more like Christ and to help us sin less.
No wonder the psalmist adds a prayer at this point:

> "Blessed are You, O LORD! Teach me
> Your statutes" (verse 12).

The psalmist had hidden God's Word in his heart and the
knowledge he does have causes him to bless God. That is
a good response. As we read the Scriptures every day, pray
that it will lead you to praise and worship God. Then the
psalmist adds a request that God would teach him His
statutes (verse 12). Oh, that we would have a similar
hunger for God's Word!

Verse 13: "With my lips I have declared all the judgments of Your mouth."

Verse 13 gives us the psalmist's third "I have" statement. Here is a third consequence of taking heed according to God's Word. The psalmist states that a proper response to God's Word is to share it with others. The psalmist used his lips to declare all the judgements of God's mouth. He obviously could not do that unless he had first sought after God and read His Word and hidden it in his heart. Having done that, now the psalmist felt compelled to pass on what he had learnt to others. What a good response to God's Word!

Our consideration of verses 11-12, focused on a personal consequence of reading God's Word – it helps us to sin less. Now the focus is on a benefit for other people from our reading of God's Word. What form declaring God's judgements takes will vary from person to person. Some are involved in public preaching. But that is not the only setting in which we can tell others things we have learnt from God's Word.

- Parents, do the things you read each day have anything of importance for you to teach your children?

- Neighbours, have the verses you have read contain anything in them that you might be able to share with your neighbour?

- What have you read that you might be able to use to help or encourage someone you come into contact with?

- If you get a fresh appreciation of the greatness of being saved, is there someone who is not a Christian you could share the Gospel with today?

THE IMPORTANCE OF GOD'S WORD

- If you found some encouragement from the Lord in some difficult circumstance, is there some family member or friend who is suffering that you could encourage today?

- If the Lord corrected some sin in your life through the Scriptures you read, might you be able to help someone who is similarly struggling with the passing pleasures of sin?

Verse 14: "I have rejoiced in the way of Your testimonies, as much as in all riches."

This is the psalmist's fourth and final "I have" statement. The point here is that reading the Scriptures is supposed to make us rejoice. That is not the same as saying that we must always be ridiculously happy with cheesy grins on our faces. Our demeanour must always be appropriate for the situation we are in. We sorrow with those who sorrow, rejoice with those who rejoice and so on (see Romans 12:15). But as we read God's Word, and as over time and by repeated reading we get a greater grasp of God's testimonies, we can rejoice as we see the wisdom of God. That means that even in trying circumstances we are able to rejoice as we read God's Word and see that He is sovereign. He is in control of all things, and that ultimately, He will do right. As we read God's instructions for how we should live, even those that are unpopular in today's culture, we can rejoice in the wisdom of God as we know that He knows what is good for us. The psalmist so valued God's Word that he rejoiced in it as much as all riches. Could we say the same thing?

We have considered four good things that the psalmist had done in the past:

1. He had sought after God with his whole heart (verse 10).
2. He had hidden God's Word in his heart (verse 11).
3. He had declared God's judgments (verse 13).
4. He had rejoiced in God's testimonies (verse 14).

He had done well in the past but that was not sufficient. He made fresh determination that day to live according to God's Word. What a good desire! Is it yours? Have we made similar determinations in our own lives? They are crucial if, like the psalmist, we want to cleanse our way.

Verses 15-16: "I will meditate on Your precepts, and [I will] contemplate Your ways. I will delight myself in Your statutes; I will not forget Your word."

Because these four statements are very similar to the "I have" statements, these two verses present us with some challenges.

• Do you meditate on God's precepts?

As you read God's Word:

• Will you contemplate what it means?
• Will you find delight in it?
• Will you remember it?

Of course, all of these questions assume that reading God's Word is a believer's regular daily experience. If it is not, start today! After all, the psalmist tells us it is the way to keep our way clean! (verse 9). You will know God's blessing as you take heed according to His Word.

ג

3. GIMEL – verses 17-24

Peter Ollerhead

Introduction

GIMEL is the third letter of the Hebrew alphabet. In verses 17-24, the psalmist records a measure of complaint when distressing circumstances, especially persecution, crowd into his life. Being a stranger in God's world there is much that puzzles, causing him to bring his anxieties to the Lord in prayer, seeking deliverance along with a deeper insight into God's ways, as revealed in His Word. There is a sense of earnest longing for that fullness of life, which is repeated time and again throughout the whole of Psalm 119.

Verse 17: "Deal bountifully with your servant, that I may live and keep your word" (ESV).

From this verse, we learn that the psalmist's prayer is for his life to be extended, not for the expected experiences of everyday living, but rather that he might have the privilege of obeying God's Word. This challenges believers over our expectations from our faith in the Lord

Jesus. Some preaching and teaching that I have encountered seems to stop at the moment we have our sins forgiven through faith in the death of Jesus. This seems to me to be a travesty of the full unfolding of the Gospel as we, quite rightly, prize the blessings of the Gospel yet, sadly, do not always grasp what John Piper calls, "the best and final gift of God's love, the gift of God's beauty."

One of the chief desires of the psalmist was to live for God and to serve Him. He will observe the teachings of Scripture because in doing so he can serve and know God, demonstrating that the very action of doing so is precious. I have long thought that a preaching that emphasises the blood of the Lord Jesus and stops short of identifying *who* Jesus is, as the incarnate Son of God, is only part of the truth. The Lord, in John 14:6, states that He is "The way." When we believe in the Lord Jesus, we enter into an experience of what the Lord calls abundant life (see John 10:10), which is superior to anything else. In measure, this is what the psalmist is longing for, though we must not read back the blessings of the Christian and apply them to the inhabitants of the Old Testament world. Their blessings were experienced in the land that God had given to them. The fifth of the Ten Commandments helps us to understand this, for it commanded the Israelite to obey and respect parents so that:

> "Your days may be long upon the land
> that the LORD your God is giving you"
> (Exodus 20:12, ESV).

Verse 18: "Open my eyes, that I may behold wondrous things out of your law" (ESV).

At first sight this prayer seems to be asking for the obvious for, if a person can read, then grasping the meaning of a sentence, or even a single word, is simple. This prayer, however, is for an acknowledgement of treasures in the Word of God, not seen by natural sight or a quick glance. It is a plea for spiritual discernment and divine unveiling to be accomplished in the psalmist by God Himself. Such a prayer is certainly in line with New Testament teaching, as we read in 1 Corinthians 2:14:

> "The natural person does not accept the things of the Spirit of God, for they are folly to him, and he is not able to understand them because they are spiritually discerned" (ESV).

The Apostle Paul enlarges and extends this thought:

> "...having the eyes of your hearts enlightened, that you may know what is the hope to which he has called you, what are the riches of his glorious inheritance in the saints" (Ephesians 1:18, ESV).

Our constant prayer should be that the Spirit of God would open the eyes of our understanding, whenever we read His Word.

I add a further extra-biblical comment upon verse 18, which is yet still relevant. We could not begin to behold wondrous things from God's Word unless we have learned to read. Universal education is a privilege that began for most English people in the latter decades of the nineteenth century. Most of us are aware that the Old

Testament Scriptures were written in Hebrew and so needed translating into our own language. I wish therefore, to draw attention to the Bible translators who are still active in this task. There are many people who still do not possess the Bible in their own languages, or dialect, and so rely upon others to provide them with portions from it. No longer are these dedicated men and women, who spend their lives translating the Scriptures, in fear of persecution and death, simply because they produce the Scriptures in a different tongue. This has not always been the case, as we can learn from the biography of William Tyndale, who was burned to death for publishing his version of the Holy Bible in English. We owe such men and women a great debt for delivering the Word of God to us in a language we can understand. Consequently, we who possess the Scriptures, have to face the challenge of verse 18 by searching for those "wondrous things".

Verse 19a: "I am a sojourner upon the earth; hide not your commandments from me!" (ESV).

Notice how the writer describes himself as a sojourner or a stranger upon the earth. This ought to be an element in our present-day Christian pathway for as Hebrews 13:14 tells us that:

> "here we have no continuing city, but we
> seek the one to come."

Though the pilgrim character of Christianity seems to be missing from many of us, it marked so many of the men and women of faith in the past. When I was young, we used to sing one of Fanny Crosby's hymns which embraces this theme:

> Whither, pilgrims, are you going,
> Going each with staff in hand?
> We are going on a journey,
> Going at our king's command.
> Over hills and plains and valleys,
> We are going to His palace,
> Going to the better land.

(Fanny J Crosby, 1820-1915)

The Apostle Paul impresses upon the Colossians the need to set their affections on things above:

> "If then you have been raised with Christ, seek the things that are above, where Christ is, seated at the right hand of God. Set your minds on things that are above, not on things that are on earth. For you have died, and your life is hidden with Christ in God" (Colossians 3:1-3, ESV).

Sadly, we find it much easier to be concerned with, and taken up by, things of time to the detriment of our spiritual life and pilgrim character.

Verses 19b-20: "Hide not your commandments from me! My soul is consumed with longing for your rules at all times" (ESV).

From this, we get a sense of the earnest desire of the psalmist for the knowledge of God's Word. Time and again throughout Psalm 119 we get expressions of a deep longing to learn more of the ways and knowledge of God, expressed in His Word. Another psalm extends this thought:

"As a deer pants for flowing streams, so pants my soul for you, O God" (Psalm 42:1, ESV).

One of the great privileges, granted to believers while dwelling in mortal flesh, is that we have knowledge of the eternal God. Paul expressed his deep longing for this to be increased:

> "Indeed, I count everything as loss because of the surpassing worth of knowing Christ Jesus my Lord. For his sake I have suffered the loss of all things and count them as rubbish, in order that I may gain Christ. ...That I may know him and the power of his resurrection and may share his sufferings, becoming like him in his death" (Philippians 3:8, 10, ESV).

When writing to the Corinthian church, Paul said that we have this knowledge in earthen vessels, in other words in our earthly bodies (see 2 Corinthians 4:7).

Verse 21:"You rebuke the insolent, accursed ones, who wander from your commandments" (ESV).

There are two points from verse 21, both of which occur time and again in Scripture. The first is the warning against insolence which, along with pride, vanity, arrogance, unrighteousness, hypocrisy, and injustice, warrants many warnings throughout the Bible. Pride appears in many guises, such as pride of place, or pride of face or pride of race – or even pride of grace, which is when we consider our spiritual knowledge is superior to others in the family of faith. The Lord Jesus warned against such an attitude when He used the comparison between the tax collector and the Pharisee in Luke 18:9-14. The Lord is the example that we should seek to follow as He said:

> "Take my yoke upon you, and learn from me, for I am gentle and lowly in heart, and you will find rest for your souls" (Matthew 11:29, ESV).

The second point is the absolute necessity for obedience. In verse 21, the psalmist warns against wandering from God's commandments, which we find extremely easy so to do. We might be able to quote whole passages of Scripture by rote, yet, until the Word of God affects our attitude and behaviour, we are not well taught Christians.

Verse 22: "Take away from me scorn and contempt, for I have kept your testimonies" (ESV).

How often verse 22 has been breathed as a prayer by many persecuted believers! Many times, during His earthly ministry, the Lord warned His disciples that they would meet opposition and ridicule. Paul repeated this warning:

> "All who desire to live godly in Christ Jesus will suffer persecution" (2 Timothy 3:12).

In some countries, that persecution can mean long periods of imprisonment or even death. It is not so serious in our land, though I am sure that we all have had to deal with contempt simply because we believe the Bible and believe that the Lord Jesus rose from the grave.

How do we deal with this mockery? Certainly not with violence, either of word or deed. I repeat that mockery and contempt is what we have been warned against by virtue of living in an unbelieving world. Generally, in the United Kingdom, our testimony to the living God, revealed in the Lord Jesus, is met with indifference, but if we do encounter scorn then let our recourse be similar to the psalmist and take the matter to the Lord in prayer. Joseph Scriven (1819-1886) penned some words that have become very well-known which might help us:

> Do thy friends despise, forsake thee?
> Take it to the Lord in prayer:
> In His arms He'll take and shield thee,
> Thou wilt find a solace there.

Some might say that such words are sentimental and simplistic. I would suggest that they are following the thought of the psalmist in verse 22.

Verse 23: "Even though princes sit plotting against me, your servant will meditate on your statutes." (ESV).

In verse 23, there is a comparison between a servant and a prince. I suppose that, all things being equal, then most of us would choose to be a prince, with all the wealth and privilege that comes with such a position. It must be stated that verse 23 is not claiming that the poor are morally superior to the rich and privileged. The touchstone must be the moral attitude and actions of a person. Here in verse 23, the one was meditating in the law of God, while the other was plotting to bring evil upon him. At the trial of the Lord Jesus, many of the influential and powerful were seeking to bring in a guilty verdict against Him. Time and again, in past years, even in our country, many servants of the Lord Jesus have been prosecuted by the state. I give three examples of men who were subject to prosecution by the magistrates:

First, William Tyndale, who suffered at the stake for translating the Scriptures into English. Despite enduring the years of tribulations as a fugitive, he continued with his God-inspired task to provide us with the Word of God, in words we could understand.

Second, John Bunyan, who suffered years in jail for simply preaching the Gospel of our Lord Jesus, when the state would not grant him permission.

Third, John Wedgwood, distantly related to Josiah Wedgwood, the famous potter. John was a preacher with the Primitive Methodists, who was also imprisoned for preaching at Grantham, without permission, in the second decade of the nineteenth century.

The writer of the Hebrew epistle was moved to quote many examples of men and women who suffered for their faith (Hebrews 11:30-37). His conclusion was that the world was not worthy of them (verse 38).

Verse 24: "Your testimonies are my delight; they are my counsellors" (ESV).

This wonderful verse also contains a challenge to us as to whether, or not, we consider God's Word a delight. The Lord had a very pertinent comment to those who were listening to Him:

> "You search the Scriptures because you think that in them you have eternal life; and it is they that bear witness about me, yet you refuse to come to me that you may have life" (John 5:39-40, ESV).

3. GIMEL – VERSES 17-24

In Luke 24:13-49 the resurrected Lord appeared to two of His disciples and:

> "expounded to them in all the Scriptures the things concerning Himself" (verse 27).

When we read the Bible, it will reveal to us the greatness and majesty of the Person of Christ, along with the wonder and immensity of His victory over death, sin and evil. These things are, or should, be a delight to us as men and women who have been brought to believe in the Lord Jesus. There is a volume, on the Christian second-hand book market, that was written by A. M. Hodgkin, entitled *Christ in all the Scriptures*[7], which I think sums up the Christian's attitude to the Bible.

Alexander MacLaren's comments, in his book on the Psalms, that the LORD's testimonies, which were the psalmist's delight (verse 24a), also "heightens the impression of the psalmist's rest":

> "Not only the subjects of his meditation, but bringing inward sweetness, though earth is in arms against him."[8]

How much inward sweetness do we gain by reading the Scriptures?

In addition, the testimonies of the Lord are our counsellors (verse 24b). Calvin stated that this was a sentence worthy to be weighed by us when the writer called the commandments of God "his counsellors." All the wisdom and pronunciations of men can be laid aside,

---

[7] Alice M. Hodgkin (1860-1955), *Christ in All the Scriptures*, London: Pickering & Inglis, 1907.

[8] Alexander MacLaren, *The Expositor's Bible; The Psalms, Volume III*, CXIX, page 252, New York: A. C. Armstrong and Sons, 1894.

when we are immersed in the Word of God, and governed by it. I believe it was Dwight Moody, the American evangelist, who said that the Bible would keep him from sin or sin would keep him from the Bible. No single statement can be the whole truth, yet there is more than an element of truth in Moody's statement. The psalmist's thought is that when he is governed by the Word, he would be truly wise. There are many ways that the Word, through the power of the Spirit, leads us into a holy life.

ד

4.   DALETH – verses 25-32

BRIAN DONALDSON

Introduction

Some commentators group the 22 stanzas of Psalm 119
into eight divisions and very helpful titles can be put over
each group. DALETH, HE, and WAW, compose the
second of these eight divisions with the theme of
'Strength for the weary'. The DALETH stanza is often
given the title of 'God's Word revives and restores'.

DALETH is generally taken to mean "door", but it also
has a sense of weak or needy and the Hebrew symbol of
it resembles a needy person who is bent over. These two
aspects therefore remind me of a tent door, pinned up at
one side to allow entry. For many of my friends and
myself this reminds us of Fenham Farm in
Northumberland, where we attended a camp at which we
stayed in canvas bell tents. When young, it was very easy
for us to stoop down and go in through the pinned-up
low tent door but as we get older it becomes more and
more of a thought! Nevertheless, it is essential to go
through the door either to go in for shelter or out into the

daylight and so it is like this stanza: we move from the previous three sections through this "door" to allow us to enjoy all that is to come later. However, just like the bell tent door at Fenham, the psalmist here is having to get down low and experience that which is perhaps difficult to face and admit to himself.

Verse 25: "My soul clings to the dust; revive me according to Your word."

The psalmist brings us back to earth after the heady spiritual contents of the previous stanza, GIMEL (verses 17-24). How easy it is for any of us to be unduly concerned and occupied with the things of earth!

We will never fully enjoy the things of God if we are earthbound. In 1 Corinthians 15 Paul teaches us about the unique place that believers in Christ are brought into as now being no longer simply following the things of the earth as descendants of Adam but, being new creatures in Christ Jesus, having a spiritual life that can lift us beyond the things of earth. 1 Corinthians 15:47 contains the wonderful expression that Adam was "of the earth, earthy." There was nothing else that he could possibly be, but as believers we have a new life that can respond to things of heaven and it is only in occupation with God's Word that we can cultivate this. The psalmist has come to this in verse 25 when he desires to be revived according to God's Word. Oh, that we may always be desiring during every aspect of life, whether good or bad, to be revived in that same way!

Verse 26: "I have declared my ways, and You answered me; teach me Your statutes."

In verse 26 the psalmist opens up to God about all his ways. Not just the good days, nor the Sundays when we go to meet with other believers for a very short period of time in comparison to the rest of our week. Not just the days when everything is going our way and life seems good. This is everything! Imagine if all my thoughts, words, actions, and deeds for just one week were made public – perhaps all displayed in the public library or published in the local paper. What a terrible thought that would be and yet the God who sees and knows everything is already overseeing our "ways" for every day of our life. After the LORD told Hagar that she would bear a son:

> "She called the name of the LORD who spoke to her, You-Are-the-God-Who-Sees; for she said, 'Have I also here seen Him who sees me?'" (Genesis 16:13).

She, too, had a great appreciation that God was watching her. So why do we need to confess our ways if God sees and knows everything anyway? Because:

> "If we confess our sins, He is faithful and just to forgive us our sins and to cleanse us from all unrighteousness" (1 John 1:9).

A tremendous verse for believers! We should never lose sight of this important teaching that seemed to be very much in the mind of the psalmist. "My ways" perhaps covers not just my faults but also the very root of sinfulness that we all have. As mentioned in verse 25, as descendants of Adam we inherited that sinful nature, and it is this that we also must lay open before God. To hide from, or ignore, our inmost nature and the sins that flow from it, means we will never be right with the holy and righteous God and enjoy His blessing in our lives. Therefore, verse 26b is a natural follow on, that having made all our ways plain to God, He has answered; and the psalmist is now free and clear to learn from God and to enjoy His promises.

Verse 27: "Make me understand the way of Your precepts; so shall I meditate on Your wonderful works."

Verse 27 is all about knowing and understanding the ways of God for ourselves before we seek to talk about them and teach others. If I were to become an expert on a secular subject, I may well be able to impart that knowledge to others without it making any difference to my own life. But in scriptural things we should first enjoy, appreciate, and put it into practice in our own lives before we teach others. Being able to teach the Scriptures is less about the knowledge gained and more about the application of that knowledge in our own lives. In Acts 17:11, the Bereans accepted what they had heard but then went and searched the Scriptures for themselves to see if these things were so. They wanted to understand fully the ways of God, so they could then meditate on the wonderful things of God. I work in Pensions and have spent many hours studying for exams to maintain a level of professional competence. Never once have I found myself meditating on the wonders of pensions, irrespective of how important they may be to me in later life! How much time do we all spend occupied with things, however innocent or needful they may be, that will never bring to us a sense of wonder and real soul satisfaction? Do you ever feel that knowledge of certain things leaves us feeling, "So what?" The study of God's Word should never leave us feeling like this. The more we understand and appreciate, the more it should make us want to praise and worship God for all that He is and all that He has done for us.

Verse 28: "My soul melts from heaviness; strengthen me according to Your word."

So, if occupation with the things of God, His ways, and His Word brings fullness and satisfaction for the soul, then verse 28 is the very opposite, occupation with self (for example, one's successes or failures, good or poor health, moans, or boastings, etc.). The psalmist uses very graphic language – his soul is melting with heaviness. Verse 25 was about the perils of being earthbound. In verse 28 it is inward looking that causes problems. What is the remedy for this? Is it to get out more and lift the spirits? Or perhaps get more exercise and eat better? Have more contact with friends or maybe take a holiday? All these things have their place, but they will never lift the soul permanently above the heaviness that the psalmist feels. He is convinced that he needs to be strengthened, uplifted, and kept by nothing other than the Word of God. The Apostle Paul reminds us of what we are at our base level (and seems to have the same view as the psalmist), when he states that the good he would like to do he cannot; and the things that he does not want to do are the very things he does:

> "O wretched man that I am!" (Romans 7:24).

If we read no further in Romans, then perhaps we would feel, like the psalmist, that our soul is "melting" with heaviness. But we should always read on into Romans 8 for the tremendous and victorious statement:

> "There is therefore now no condemnation to those who are in Christ Jesus" (8:1).

I believe this will lift our spirits above all the challenges of this life. Remember this promise of God when you are feeling down.

Verse 29: "Remove from me the way of lying and grant me Your law graciously."

Verse 29 raises the simple question as to whether we are prepared to accept the truth about our ourselves or whether we will deny it. We may very well be the kind of person who would never intentionally lie to someone about something important. But what about to the all-knowing God about things that, perhaps, no other person knows about? An example of this might be projecting oneself as having it all together spiritually, yet inwardly being spiritually very dry. God hates lying! He wants us to be truthful in every aspect of our lives, He wants truth in the inner man (see Psalm 51:6). Paul desired that we might be strengthened by the Holy Spirit in the inner man (Ephesians 3:16).

How could this possibly work if we are not being truthful with ourselves, with others, and with God?

Verse 29b: "Grant me Your law graciously."

The psalmist makes this interesting request after desiring that the way of lying might be removed (verse 29a). Grace and law do not mix very well:

4. DALETH – verses 25-32

"The law was given by Moses, but grace
and truth came by Jesus Christ" (John
1:17, KJV).

There was nothing wrong with God's law. It was given by
Him to make His people realise how holy He was and
how far short they had become. Paul refers to the law as
a "tutor to bring us to Christ" (Galatians 3:24).

There is no contradiction between these verses and Psalm
119:29b for the literal Hebrew translation is: "Favour me
with Your law."

The children of Israel were favoured by God to be given
His law yet what a burden it became for them! How
different for those who are in Christ – we can seek God's
favour and blessing by doing His work and will because
of what Christ has done for us. Paul reminded the
Ephesian believers that it is by grace they were saved (see
Ephesians 2:8). So for Christians, to serve and worship
God should be a privilege and not a chore.

Verse 30: "I have chosen the way of truth; Your judgments I have laid before me."

After he has looked inside himself and given himself
some tough challenges, the psalmist's mind is made up
and he is determined to follow the way of truth.
However, this decision is not the end of the story for him
or for his journey. And when a person accepts Christ, they
should feel the same. Yes, we are then fit and ready for
heaven, but meanwhile we must prepare ourselves for
what will lie ahead in this life whether long or short. We
can only do this by having the Scriptures before us
regularly in the same way as the psalmist was determined
to do for himself. I have already referred to the Bereans

THE IMPORTANCE OF GOD'S WORD

(Acts 17:11). Similarly, Paul urged his young friend Timothy to study the Word so that he would be approved and unashamed as a workman for God (see 2 Timothy 2:15). In a day and age when this world seems to admire many things that are not true and are very definitely wrong, we should be marked as rejoicing in that which is honest and true. One of my favourite verses of Scripture is Philippians 4:8, where the Apostle Paul urges believers to think on various things which will be good for them; the first three of these things are true, noble, and just.

Verse 31: "I cling to Your testimonies; O LORD, do not put me to shame!"

Whilst verse 30 presented the psalmist's determination, verse 31 shows his devotion. He is now using the same word as used in verse 25 (when he was clinging to the dust) to show he is now clinging to the Word of God. What a change in his outlook as he moves through the door to the blessing of God! As mentioned above, Paul encouraged Timothy to study so that he might properly teach God's Word. There is nothing worse when those who profess to teach Bible truth put forward views and beliefs that are at complete odds with the very thing they are teaching. How sad, but God will not be mocked. He will put all things right and be vindicated in a day to come. There is also another aspect of verse 31 which is similar to verse 30. If when the ways of God, the Scriptures, His testimonies are laid before us and we choose to walk in them, they will keep us in the way of righteousness. Therefore we will avoid the shame brought to those who do not make this choice.

We all are disappointed and feel let down when we see or hear of people whom we once held in respect shamed by one scandal or another. With today's social media, very few things remain secret for very long. Sometimes just one off-guard moment and the shame that the psalmist wants to avoid can be brought upon us. However, what the court of public opinion may consider "shame" is not necessarily the same as what God considers shameful. Many aspects of life this world now finds acceptable are contrary to God's standards. We should always hold to His unalterable standards and not those of this present age.

Verse 32: "I will run the course of Your commandments, for You shall enlarge my heart."

In verse 32, we see the one who began this stanza burdened, earthbound and rather depressed in his soul, now metaphorically running – with his heart enlarged and beating hard with the wonder of the things of God. This is a slightly different thought to when the Apostle Paul could write in 2 Timothy 4:7 about finishing the race. That is more to do with the life Paul had lived. In verse 32, it is more the thought of running through the course that God has set the psalmist according to His ways. It is like standing at the start of an obstacle course with many different things to contend with but knowing that we have the strength to deal with each one as it comes up. So all the challenges that God gives us to encourage us, build us up and bring us into blessing, like the psalmist, we should be prepared to take them on with vigour and enthusiasm. The psalmist was willing to let the ways of God run freely throughout his life, knowing that he can only do so by the Lord enlarging his heart.

The King James Version says: "I will run the way of thy commandments, when thou shalt enlarge my heart", or:

"I will...when You..." But the New King James Version makes us see that it is more: "I will...because You have...".

It seems that all the ways of God are coursing through his veins, like the very blood that keeps us alive and makes us move physically. It is the Word of God that gets him up in the morning; it is this that gives him the enthusiasm to live life in all its fullness. The ways of God have become the psalmist's life blood. What is it that makes you or me feel alive? What is the main motivating factor in your or my life? What a challenge this surely is for each one of us!

ה

5.   HE – verses 33-40

David G Pulman

Introduction

Each verse in this fifth stanza commences, in the original
Hebrew Scriptures, with the Hebrew letter HE, the fifth
letter in the Hebrew alphabet. The meaning of the letter
HE is a window, lattice window or an opening. So, we
have the thought of looking, beholding, contemplating,
and giving access to light – as in verse 130:

> "The entrance of Your words gives light;
> it gives understanding [or instruction] to
> the simple [or those who do not know the
> truth]."

Psalm 119 is all about God's law and most of the verses
reference the word 'law' or one of its synonyms, such as
statutes.

Each verse in this fifth stanza is a couplet and as we
consider each verse, we will see how both parts
complement each other.

Finally, some scholars believe that these eight verses could be considered as a prayer. We will see that this is most appropriate as we briefly study the verses one by one.

Verse 33: "Teach me, O LORD, the way of Your statutes, and I shall keep it to the end."

"Teach me…" tell us immediately about the psalmist, the desire of his heart, and the value he places upon God's Word. His plea goes directly to God with the expression "O LORD."

"The way of your statutes" is a slightly strange expression, but the psalmist is willing to learn. The statutes will give instruction for the journey of life. So, in the opening words of the stanza we have someone with an open heart, a mind ready to learn and live by God's Word.

"And I shall keep it to the end" is the second part of this verse which emphasises the lifelong commitment.

2 Timothy 3:16 states:

> "All Scripture is given by inspiration of God, and is profitable for doctrine, for reproof, for correction, for instruction in righteousness."

In 2 Timothy 3:16 Paul is seeking to remind Timothy of the value and importance of all and every Scripture. This parallels the longing of the psalmist to be taught by God's Word. Paul was acutely aware of the living power of God's Word. These verses are a challenge to every Christian to know and live by God's instruction in righteousness.

We have started this stanza with the psalmist's intense desire and longing to be taught. The recognition that God's Word is the only true source of instruction enables a fullness in a committed life.

Verse 34: "Give me understanding, and I shall keep Your law; indeed, I shall observe it with my whole heart."

Verse 34 is a step forward, not only is there a desire to be taught (verse 33), but the need to understand what is being taught – "give me understanding". Christians are expected to understand the Bible so that it will have the right kind of impact on their lives. We need to prayerfully read the Bible, to understand the Scriptures in their context, and where it is right to do so, apply its teaching to our lives. Part of Solomon's personal prayer to God was for understanding:

> "Therefore give to Your servant an
> understanding heart to judge Your people,
> that I may discern between good and evil"
> (1 Kings 3:9).

No matter how well we are taught, if we do not understand the relevance of the teaching then we will not be able to apply what we have learned. (Solomon was able to do this concerning the two women who both laid claim to the same child [see 1 Kings 3:16-28]). This puts a great burden upon Bible teachers to speak and write with clarity.

With understanding the psalmist was confident that he would "keep Your law" (verse 34). This reminds me of "Terms and Conditions" attached to many products and services. They are so often lengthy and lacking in clarity that many people simply ignore them. It only becomes an issue when something goes wrong!

Verse 34b: "I shall observe it with my whole heart."

Here we see the enthusiasm of the psalmist. It was Ezra who committed himself to be a teacher in Israel:

> "For Ezra had prepared his heart to seek the Law of the LORD, and to do it, and to teach statutes and ordinances in Israel" (Ezra 7:10).

This kind of attitude needs to be the same for every believer. In Nehemiah 8, Ezra read from the law to all the assembled people in Jerusalem. As he read the Scriptures, there were others with him who helped the people to understand what was being read (see Nehemiah 8:8). Ezra had help in his mission to teach the people. This must be the same in assemblies and fellowships – that more than one person needs to show Christian responsibility for teaching and enabling all believers to understand and to grow spiritually.

In Luke 24:13-49 the Lord Jesus helps the two disciples travelling home to Emmaus:

> "He [the risen Lord] opened their understanding, that they might comprehend the Scriptures" (Luke 24:45).

The Lord Jesus also spoke about the Holy Spirit that:

> "When He, the Spirit of truth, has come, He will guide you into all truth" (John 16:13).

Verse 35: "Make me walk in the path of Your commandments, for I delight in it."

Again, the psalmist is not only prepared to live his life in obedience to the Scriptures, but he also appreciates his own weakness. So, he asks for assistance from the only One who can truly give the necessary help – "make me". This life of obedience is the psalmist's delight, his pleasure. There is nothing else in the whole world that comes anywhere near to giving real delight and pleasure:

> "Blessed is the man who walks not in the counsel of the ungodly, nor stands in the path of sinners, nor sits in the seat of the scornful; but his delight is in the law of the LORD, and in His law, he meditates day and night" (Psalm 1:1-2).

Do I have such pleasure in being obedient to God's Word? This is a very real challenge. Am I in the right spiritual frame of mind? Let us not forget about the word "command". A command is a clear instruction to do something. There are no options and no alternatives. One of the Ten Commandments states:

> "You shall not murder" (Exodus 20:13).

The Commandments that apply to our relationships with other people are good principles to live by. Now they are not only in the Old Testament, but also in the New Testament. Romans 13:9-10 state:

> "You shall not commit adultery, you shall not murder, you shall not steal, you shall not bear false witness, you shall not covet, and if there is any other commandment, are all summed up in this saying, namely,

> you shall love your neighbour as yourself.
> Love does no harm to a neighbour;
> therefore, love is the fulfilment of the
> law."

Just think what the world would be like if everyone followed this teaching, but unbelievers will not because it is contrary to their unregenerate nature. However, Christians are expected to follow the teaching of Paul in Romans 13:9-10. The Bible is our instruction manual for righteous living. John states:

> "I have no greater joy than to hear that my
> children walk in truth" (3 John 4).

The teaching of Psalm 119 is very relevant to Christians as it parallels New Testament teaching regarding faithfulness to God's Word.

Verse 36: "Incline my heart to Your testimonies, and not to covetousness."

This may seem an odd couplet, not like verses 33-35. However, the LORD speaks about the heart of the natural man, through His servant Jeremiah:

> "The heart is deceitful above all things,
> and desperately wicked: who can know
> it?" (Jeremiah 17:9).

I am sure that the psalmist was equally aware of the tendency of the heart to stray after wrong things, so he desires that his heart be inclined or lean towards God's word. God's testimonies are those stanzas that witness to God's holy nature, His purposes, His heart of love, and His unswerving righteousness. It is an unwritten requirement that we should be ever mindful of who God is.

We are not to major on God's love at the expense of God's righteousness and holiness. We are to be rightly balanced Christians. Covetousness is associated with desiring anything that is not legitimately mine and is the tenth commandment:

"You shall not covet..." (Exodus 20:17).

Therefore, the psalmist wants the positive, of leaning towards God's Word, and to be kept from the negative, covetousness. Covetousness is listed among attributes of the godless in both Mark 7:20-23 and Romans 1:28-32. In Mark, wickedness springs from the heart and in Romans it comes from the mind. We see that the unsaved person is only evil in his ways and God will judge such unless they turn to the Lord Jesus Christ and receive Him truly as their Saviour.

Verse 37: "Turn away my eyes from looking at worthless things, and revive me in Your way."

In life we cannot help but see things that are "worthless". They are not of any spiritual or moral value – things that are negative as far as the Christian lifestyle is concerned. But we can refrain from "looking", a scriptural word which means to have a good look, seeking to observe all the detail! This is a real challenge in a world that seeks to promote wrong values and images. The psalmist wants the 'real' life to be dominant in his life; this is the godly life, which has its origin in God. This life has a purpose. It is to keep the godly on the right pathway.

Early believers were known by the term "the Way" or "that Way" (see Acts 9:2, 19:9, 19:23, 24:14, 24:22). The expression not only indicated a journey but the type of journey. This journey had resulted from their encounter

with the Lord Jesus Christ, accepting Him as their Saviour
and Lord. This experience changed their lives and people
could see the change. The psalmist has the same desire; he
wanted to live God's way. In Genesis 4:1-5:32, there is the
record of a man called Enoch. One of the outstanding
features of Enoch is that he walked with God (Genesis
5:22, 24.) He was a man who had been revived in God's
way.

These words are challenging. Does my life show that I am
a Christian? Or does my life blend into the crowd so that
I become indistinguishable from the people around me?

Verse 38: "Establish Your word to Your servant, who is devoted to fearing You."

The first part of verse 38 seems to imply that we need to
have the Word of God firmly fixed in our hearts and
minds. Paul encourages believers to be "rooted and
grounded in love" (Ephesians 3:17). In other words, to
gain nourishment from divine love and to have love as a
solid foundation on which to build their lives. It is similar
in Psalm 119:38. The desire of the psalmist is that God's
Word be established in his life – that God would make the
Word unchangeable and totally reliable. Why does he ask
such a thing? Because the psalmist holds God in the
highest esteem. God is the Sovereign of the universe. In
His hand He holds the life and existence of all creation.
There is to be no lightness, or frivolity, of attitude
concerning God. Christians do not carelessly use the
name of God, or the name of Jesus, as unbelievers do. It
is so easy to fall into the ways and language of the world.
Let us guard our lips and tongue.

Verse 39: "Turn away my reproach which I dread, for Your judgments are good."

There is one single certainty that every true Christian can expect from this godless world and that is ridicule, mockery, and reproach. Being faithful to the Lord Jesus Christ will bring such a response from others. There is also another sadness that I have observed: that when a believer endeavours to obey God's instruction, fellow believers ridicule and mock because they do not feel the need to obey what God has written.

The other thought that may have been in the mind of the psalmist is his fear of failure. Failure would bring reproach upon the psalmist and it would reflect badly upon his God. Failure and lack of faithfulness is damaging to the testimony and brings dishonour to God.

This is balanced by the psalmist referring to God's judgments because they are good as indeed is the whole of God's Word. God's judgments are His decisions upon persons, and/or things, that are based upon His assessment. God's assessment will always be true. Therefore, if God has made a judgment then it is imperative that we as believers abide by that decision. We agree with God even if it runs totally contrary to the current trends of the day.

Verse 40: "Behold, I long for Your precepts; revive me in Your righteousness."

The psalmist is making a declaration of a past decision; it has not changed in his heart, but he requires a fresh reviving. A precept is that which is a specific charge for which we are expected to be responsible. In Ephesians 5:25 we have stated that husbands are to love their wives.

If I look around in this world, I see that this is often regarded as a temporary precept; it would place no lasting responsibility, or commitment, upon me as a husband. If on the other hand I consider God's Word, then it is binding upon me while my wife and I are both living. I am expected to love regardless of situations that we may experience in our lives together. From this scriptural illustration I can see that a precept is important. There are many precepts in God's Word that apply to me. We can therefore see how the psalmist wants to be re-invigorated in God's righteousness. He wants to live right according to God's principles.

Conclusions

I have mentioned that some Bible teachers consider this stanza as a prayer. I think we could consider each verse as a short prayer.

Please note that one Hebrew word may be translated by more than one English word: 'teach me', 'give me understanding', 'make me walk', 'incline', 'turn away', 'establish', 'turn away' and 'behold'. Remember the Hebrew letter HE has the meaning of a window or an opening. Therefore, we can see how these verses speak of letting God's Word have an entrance into our hearts and minds: "The entrance of Your words gives light" (verse 130). How much of God's Word are we allowing into our lives?

A chorus that was taught to young children in Sunday School was simple but highly instructive:

> Read your Bible, read your Bible,
> Read it daily, read it daily,
> It's a lamp, it's a lamp,
> And a light to your pathway.

What was good instruction for young children is still an important message for people of every age. Read it, do it daily, it illuminates the soul and makes clear the path we must walk in this world for God's glory.

ו

6. WAW – verses 41-48

David Anderson

Introduction

Each verse of this stanza of the psalm begins with the Hebrew letter WAW. In the original Hebrew text, verses 41-48 are a sequence of thoughts joined by the conjunction WAW (English, "and"). But in English versions of the Scriptures WAW is not always translated "and". For example, verse 42 begins with the word 'then', or 'so'.

Verse 41: "Let your steadfast love come to me, O LORD, your salvation according to your promise" (ESV).

This verse continues the prayerful theme of many previous verses of Psalm 119, especially the prior stanza, HE (verses 33-40). The psalmist continues to ask the LORD to assist him to live a godly life. He commenced this psalm:

> "Blessed are those whose way is blameless, who walk in the law of the

LORD! Blessed are those who keep his testimonies, who seek him with their whole heart, who also do no wrong, but walk in his ways! You have commanded your precepts to be kept diligently" (verses 1-4, ESV).

In verse 41, he shows that the godly rely upon the LORD's steadfast love to be blessed. Whilst this love is extended in a general way to all mankind (see Psalm 36:7), the godly personally experience, and benefit from, it. 'Steadfast love' is variously translated:

- 'Unfailing love' (NIV).
- 'Kindness' (YLT) or 'loving kindness(es)' (Darby and American Standard Version[9]).
- 'Mercy' (Brenton[10]) or 'mercies' (RV and KJV).

Steadfast love is a love that will never turn away from you nor let you down! When translated 'mercy/mercies' it indicates that the LORD's love also provides for our short-comings.

The psalmist addressed God, "O LORD" – the living God revealed to Israel as the great "I AM" (see Exodus 3:14). God's steadfast love was the theme of the praises of Israel, especially at high points in the nation's history. For example, at the dedication of the temple they sang: "For he is good, for his steadfast love endures forever" (2 Chronicles 5:13).

[9] *The Holy Bible containing the Old and New Testaments translated out of the original tongues : being the version set forth A.D. 1611 compared with the most ancient authorities and revised.* New York: Thomas Nelson & Sons, 1911.
[10] *The Septuagint Version of the Old Testament, Translated into English* by Sir Lancelot Charles Lee Brenton, London: Samuel Bagster and Sons, 1844.

In this Christian dispensation, believers know God as the Father, whose great love has been fully revealed to us in the person of His Son, Jesus Christ.

There was a special way in which the psalmist was in great need of the LORD's steadfast love, which he calls, "your salvation". Throughout Psalm 119, the psalmist elaborated upon the many dangers which the godly encounter:

- The fear of not practically living up to his professed faith in God, especially during times of illness (verses 6-8, 29-31, 67, 83, 92, 101 133, 143, 153-154, 176).

- His concern of slipping into evil ways due to the ongoing problem of sin within his heart despite his repulsion of it (verses 9-11, 36, 104, 163).

- The attractiveness of things of the world, which are really of no lasting value (verse 37).

- The loneliness of being a pilgrim (verses 19-20, 126-128, 136, 139).

- The reproach, scorn, contempt, false accusations, oppression, and persecution from ungodly people, including worldly authorities (verses 21-23, 39, 61, 69-70, 77-78, 86-87, 95, 98, 107, 110, 115, 118-119, 121, 134, 141, 150, 157, 161).

The last danger is the predominant danger. It is also identified in many other psalms because the world is in open opposition to God, and consistently targets the godly. In reality, the world never changes, and all of these dangers continue for believers today. If anything, matters are getting worse as a reading of Open Doors' most recent *World Watch* will demonstrate. This intensity of opposition to God will only increase as the world heads towards those last days identified in Psalm 2:1-3 (ESV):

> "Why do the nations rage and the peoples plot in vain? The kings of the earth set themselves, and the rulers take counsel together, against the LORD and against his Anointed, saying, 'Let us burst their bonds apart and cast away their cords from us.'"

It will be in those last days that the godly remnant of Israel will use prayers (such as Psalm 119:41) which are found throughout the entire Book of Psalms.

Believers from every dispensation can pray these prayers and receive God's salvation, whatever the problems are that assail them – persecution, illness, disease, isolation, bereavement, difficult circumstances, etc. (compare Romans 8:18, 26-28). The salvation in verse 41 is about deliverance from problems or being sustained through them. It is not about salvation from the judgment of God. That is an already settled issue for believers. Note also, that this deliverance is "according to your promise [or your word]". "*According to*" is a repetitive phrase throughout the entire Psalm:

> "How can a young man keep his way pure? By guarding it *according to* your word" (verse 9).

> "My soul clings to the dust; give me life *according to* your word" (verse 25).

> "My soul melts away for sorrow; strengthen me *according to* your word" (verse 28).

"I entreat your favour with all my heart; be gracious to me *according to* your promise" (verse 58).

"You have dealt well with your servant, O LORD, *according to* your word" (verse 65).

"Let your steadfast love comfort me *according to* your promise to your servant" (verse 76).

"I am severely afflicted; give me life, O LORD, *according to* your word" (verse 107).

"Uphold me *according to* your promise, that I may live, and let me not be put to shame in my hope" (verse 116).

"Keep steady my steps *according to* your promise, and let no iniquity get dominion over me" (verse 133).

"Plead my cause and redeem me; give me life *according to* your promise" (verse 154).

"Let my plea come before you; deliver me *according to* your word" (verse 170).

The psalmist had faith in God's Word and in the many promises of salvation it contains. Psalm 91 is about Messiah and how God protected Him during His life upon earth as the devil acknowledged at the Lord's Temptations (see Luke 4:9-13). Here are some of its promises, which we, too, can rely on:

"He who dwells in the shelter of the Most High will abide in the shadow of the Almighty. I will say to the LORD, 'My refuge and my fortress, my God, in whom

I trust.' For he will deliver you from the snare of the fowler and from the deadly pestilence. ... 'Because he holds fast to me in love, I will deliver him; I will protect him, because he knows my name. When he calls to me, I will answer him; I will be with him in trouble; I will rescue him and honour him. With long life I will satisfy him and show him my salvation'" (Psalm 91:1-3, 14-16, ESV).

One final point on the promises of God. "All the promises of God find their Yes in [Christ]" (2 Corinthians 1:20). Therefore Paul was confident in his assertion that, with respect to dangers, God has delivered us in the past; He does deliver us now; and He will deliver us in the future (see 2 Corinthians 1:10). To which we add our "Amen!"

Verse 42: "Then shall I have an answer for him who taunts me, for I trust in your word" (ESV).

The psalmist knew that God would answer his request for salvation (verse 41). The consequence was that he would be able to defend his faith in the LORD against anybody who taunted him. Most translations suggest the idea of being reproached for simply trusting in God. An extended meaning is to pull down the believer's faith and to carp at him and in so doing, to speak against God or blaspheme. This is the predominant danger that the psalmist faced (see verse 41). Perhaps, the psalmist intuitively knew that it was not himself but the LORD who was being targeted. But he felt that he was in danger of being completely overwhelmed: "My zeal consumes me, because my foes forget your words" (verse 139).

How comforting and reassuring it is to know that God's Word has the answer in these difficult situations; and to know that you will be given the right thing to say in response to those who attack you and your faith in God and His Word.

Christian believers encounter many such opposers these days:

- Cynical evolutionists, who deride those of us who believe that God instantly created all things by the word of His power. We are dismissed as being 'unscientific' when the opposite charge is true! The answer we have to these cynics is found in Genesis 1-2 and other passages of Scripture such as John 1, Colossians 1, and Hebrews 1.

- Aggressive secular atheists, who match the description of the fool in Psalm 14:1-4, who "says in his heart, 'There is no God.' They are corrupt, they do abominable deeds; there is none who does good. The LORD looks down from heaven on the children of man, to see if there are any who understand, who seek after God. They have all turned aside; together they have become corrupt; there is none who does good, not even one. Have they no knowledge, all the evildoers who eat up my people as they eat bread and do not call upon the LORD?"

The advice of Peter is:

> "But sanctify in your hearts Christ as Lord: being ready always to give answer to every man that asks you a reason concerning the hope that is in you, yet

with meekness and fear" (1 Peter 3:15, RV).

Hebrews 12:3 states:

> "Therefore, if you would escape becoming weary and faint-hearted, compare your own sufferings with those of Him [the Lord Jesus] who endured such hostility directed against Him by sinners" (Weymouth New Testament[11]).

Verse 43: "And take not the word of truth utterly out of my mouth, for my hope is in your rules" (ESV).

Verse 43 is more or less a repeat of the prayer of verse 41. But the emphasis is on the psalmist's expressed utter dependence on the truth found in God's Word. His prayer is the practical consequence of considering those who are so vocal in their derision of the godly and of God himself. What hope of survival has he outside of believing and following God's Word? How can he objectively know what is right and what is wrong in situations where people discard the truth and embrace/promote error, with the accompanying promotion of evil? This is very much a real issue for the faithful in the so-called 'enlightened' twenty-first century. Like the psalmist of old, our only hope is in God's Word – His rules, that is, what He states to be right and to be wrong. Other translations call these "judgments" (Darby and KJV) to convey the meaning that these are divine pronouncements, which are clearly stated in unmistakable terms. The psalmist put his hope in them, in the

---

[11] Richard Francis Weymouth, *The New Testament in Modern Speech*, London: James Clarke & Co., 1903.

THE IMPORTANCE OF GOD'S WORD

knowledge that everybody will have to give account of themselves to God at His judgment seat (see Romans 14:11-12).

Verses 44-45: "I will keep your law continually, forever and ever, and I shall walk in a wide place, for I have sought your precepts" (ESV).

Verses 44-48 exude with renewed confidence in the LORD and a determination to be pious. Four times the psalmist says, "I will..." and twice, "I shall..."

Verses 44-45 form one sentence. Verse 44 expresses the psalmist's commitment based on his confidence that the LORD will do what he requested in verse 43. The psalmist committed to keeping the Law – always, as a continual habit and adds forever and ever – to emphasise the seriousness of his vow. He promised to guard and to attend to all the demands of the Law, the Torah. Strict observation of the Law marked out the godly in Israel. Whenever I read through the Pentateuch, I always think how difficult it must have been to remember all the details of it, never mind total compliance! But the Lord Jesus did say that He had come to fulfil it – every iota and dot of it (see Matthew 5:17-18). He did much more than that; He magnified it and made it honourable (see Isaiah 42:21)! He was the only One who could and did. Nevertheless, the psalmist's attitude and commitment are both admirable and correct.

In verse 45, to "walk in a wide place" is to have liberty to keep the Law, to be free to serve God – to have liberty to speak about Him (verse 42) and to live for Him (verse 43). David similarly experienced the LORD's salvation:

"[The LORD] brought me out into a broad place; he rescued me, because he delighted in me. The LORD dealt with me according to my righteousness; according to the cleanness of my hands he rewarded me" (Psalm 18:19-20, ESV).

With respect to Christian believers, the Lord Jesus insists that we must obey His commandments.[12] The Apostle John assures us that these commandments are not burdensome (see 1 John 5:3). Romans 6:20-22 state that Christian believers have been set free from sin to serve God. The Lord Jesus told the Jews who had "believed" in Him that His Word is the power for this liberty:

"If you abide in my word, you are truly my disciples, and you will know the truth, and the truth will set you free. ...Truly, truly, I say to you, everyone who practices sin is a slave to sin. The slave does not remain in the house forever; the son remains forever. So if the Son sets you free, you will be free indeed" (John 8:31-32, 34-36, ESV).

Commenting on verse 45, Matthew Henry wrote:

"The service of sin is perfect slavery. But, the service of God is perfect liberty!"[13]

[12] John 14:15, 21, John 15:10 with 1 John 2:3 and 1 John 3:22, 24.
[13] Matthew Henry (1662-1714), *An Exposition of the Old and New Testaments, Volume III-II - Psalm XCI to Song of Solomon*, 1706-1721.

The

Verse 46: "I will also speak of your testimonies before kings and shall not be put to shame" (ESV).

The psalmist is now confident in God's salvation and brave in his testimony. He now sees himself walking in the liberty of saints who have complete confidence in God's salvation. He is delivered from the fear of man and knows that he will not feel ashamed even when he testifies before kings, who may not acknowledge God's authority. Think of those saints who actually stood before kings:

- Daniel and his three friends who risked their lives before Nebuchadnezzar and Darius (Daniel chapters 3 & 6).

- The Apostle Paul's testimonies before King Agrippa (Acts 25:13-27), Festus (Acts 25:1-9) and Felix (Acts 24:10-21). He wrote:

  "For I am not ashamed of the gospel, for it is the power of God for salvation to everyone who believes. ...For with the heart man believes unto righteousness; and with the mouth confession is made unto salvation" (Romans 1:16 and 10:10).

Verse 47: "For I find my delight in your commandments, which I love" (ESV).

Verse 47 gives the reason why the psalmist is so bold. Because his heart is full of delight in, and love for, it he can:

- Speak God's Word (verse 43).

- Live a life that exemplifies it (verses 44-45).

74

- Give faithful witness to God from it (verse 46).

These thoughts are expressed throughout Psalm 119 and in other psalms, for example:

> "The law of the LORD is perfect, reviving the soul; the testimony of the LORD is sure, making wise the simple; the precepts of the LORD are right, rejoicing the heart; the commandment of the LORD is pure, enlightening the eyes; the fear of the LORD is clean, enduring forever; the rules of the LORD are true, and righteous altogether. More to be desired are they than gold, even much fine gold; sweeter also than honey and drippings of the honeycomb. Moreover, by them is your servant warned; in keeping them there is great reward" (Psalm 19:7-11, ESV).

Verse 48: "I will lift up my hands toward your commandments, which I love, and I will meditate on your statutes" (ESV).

Verse 48 concludes this stanza with two more "I will's". This verse conveys the psalmist's reverence for God. The whole tenor of it is an attitude of worship. It also indicates that he was determined to maintain his godliness by prayerful *meditation* on God's Word, a statement which is repeated throughout Psalm 119:

- "I will *meditate* on your precepts and fix my eyes on your ways" (verse 15).

- "Your servant will *meditate* on your statutes" (verse 23).

- "Make me understand the way of your precepts, and I will *meditate* on your wondrous works" (verse 27).

- "As for me, I will *meditate* on your precepts" (verse 78).

- "Oh how I love your law! It is my *meditation* all the day" (verse 97).

- "I have more understanding than all my teachers, for your testimonies are my *meditation*" (verse 99).

- "My eyes are awake before the watches of the night, that I may *meditate* on your promise" (verse 148).

It has already been stated that Psalm 2 gives the prophetic context of the Psalms. Psalm 1:1-2 describe the stark distinction that will exist in those days between the godly and the ungodly:

> "Blessed is the [godly] man who walks not in the counsel of the [ungodly], nor stands in the way of sinners, nor sits in the seat of scoffers; but his delight is in the law of the LORD, and on his law he meditates day and night" (ESV).

As we approach those times, you and I will only be equipped to live for the Lord if we too, like the psalmist, love, delight in, and meditate upon God's Word. Meditation means that our minds are constantly full of God's Word so that our thoughts and actions are in tune with it. So, are we experiencing God's daily deliverance by His Word; and are we willing to serve the Lord?

Finally, a prayer of similar words to verse 48 found in Psalm 19:14:

> "May the words of our mouths and the meditation of our hearts on your word always be acceptable in your sight, O LORD, our rock and our redeemer." Amen!

ז

7.   ZAIN – verses 49-56

Paul Thomson

Introduction

ZAIN with CHETH and TETH, the next two stanzas in Psalm 119, form a whole division (verses 49-72) which could be headed, "Our immense spiritual riches."

The shape of the Hebrew letter ZAIN resembles a hand-held weapon. Every Christian's weapon is "the sword of the Spirit, which is the Word of God" (Ephesians 6:17).

The Word of God (the Bible) explains how to be equipped for the spiritual battle we face daily as well as assuring us of God's precious promises. Today, more than ever, the Christian needs to be laying hold of the Bible which equips him or her with everything they need for every circumstance they will face in this world.

The name of the author of Psalm 119 is not given but it is most probably David. (But no matter who the writer is, we can hear God's voice speaking in every verse.) Assuming it was David, he was a young man in 1 Samuel 17 who, under his father's instruction, went to see how his brothers were doing in the war with the Philistines (verses 17-22). David found out that the whole of Israel was afraid because they were being challenged by a mighty warrior, a giant called Goliath (verses 23-25). No-one had the courage or ability to fight Goliath because he was so big and mighty. David was a youth with no experience of war; what could he do? Not very much according to his brothers and King Saul. But David stepped up to the battle with experience and confidence, not in himself but in his God (verse 37). David had previous experience of God saving him from the paw of the lion and the paw of the bear as he watched his father's sheep in the hill country (verses 1-22). Saul gave David his armour, but this was no use to David as he had never proved it (verses 38-39). David had proved his God! (verse 37) Goliath ridiculed David as he saw him coming toward him (verse 42). But David went forward with confidence "running" (verse 48) to meet Goliath "in the name of the LORD of hosts" (verse 45), which speaks to us of the One who is mighty in battle, and David killed the giant (verse 50).

This amazing story has been told to children and adults so many times, but have you ever put yourself in David's shoes? No doubt you have faced many issues or foes in your life, maybe not all as blatant as a Goliath. But how have you approached them? In your own strength or by taking hold of the thousands of promises that God has made to us in His Word, then drawing strength and confidence from what God says. David was a man after God's own heart (see Acts 13:23), who loved the Word of God and spent much time meditating on it. May this story encourage you to use the weapon God has given you, the Bible, so by reading it you gain confidence and trust in God.

Verse 49: "Remember the word unto thy servant, upon which thou hast caused me to hope" (KJV).

In verse 49, the psalmist prays a prayer of love, asking not to be forgotten because he is conscious of his insignificance and anxious never to be overlooked. The basis of this prayer is reminding God of what He has said and promised. The psalmist asks for no new promises or deliverance from the affliction he mentions (verse 50). The psalmist claims hope as he meditates on the powerful promises of God. Annie Johnson Flint (1866-1932) wrote a beautiful poem which is apt for this verse:

> God hath not promised skies ever blue,
> Flower-strewn pathways all our lives through;
> God hath not promised sun without rain,
> Joy without sorrow, peace without pain.
>
> But God hath promised strength for the day,
> Rest for the labour, light for the way,
> Grace for the trials, help from above,
> Unfailing sympathy, undying love.
>
> God hath not promised we shall not know
> Toil and temptation, trouble and woe;
> He hath not told us we shall not bear
> Many a burden, many a care.
>
> God hath not promised smooth roads and wide,
> Swift, easy travel, needing no guide;
> Never a mountain, rocky and steep,
> Never a river, turbid and deep.

You can read all the precious promises of God but unless you appropriate them by faith you will never be in the good of them. It is an interesting thought that in prayer, as the psalmist did, we should remind God of His promises to us.

Verse 50: "This is my comfort in my affliction: for thy word hath quickened me" (KJV).

In verse 50, the psalmist finds the comfort he needs in the Word of God. It is interesting to note that he does not ask for deliverance from his affliction. We are not told of the affliction he has but it is obviously a personal one as he says, "my affliction." The challenge has got to be: what is your comfort in times of personal affliction? In verse 107, the psalmist goes further when he says to the LORD:

> "I am afflicted very much: quicken me, O LORD, according to thy word" (KJV).

I suggest that such experiences teach us how to pray!

The Apostle Paul had an affliction which he asked God on three occasions to remove but he was told that it would not be removed (see 2 Corinthians 12:7-10). But Paul found comfort in God:

> "For the which cause I also suffer these things: nevertheless, I am not ashamed: for I know whom I have believed, and am persuaded that He is able to keep that which I have committed unto Him against that day" (2 Timothy 1:12, KJV).

The Lord promised: "I will not leave you comfortless: I will come to you" (John 14:18, KJV).

Comfort in affliction is like a lamp in a dark place.

The psalmist goes on to speak of quickening; what does that mean? To quicken means to live, to revive, or to bring back to life. We are no different to the psalmist; afflictions and circumstances in life get us down. But if we apply God's Word to our circumstances, we will look on things with a whole new perspective. On a foggy morning it is impossible for us to clear away the fog so we can see things more clearly, but God has the power to do it. Have you ever experienced taking off in an aeroplane in the fog? It can be quite frightening! As you take off, you see nothing but when you rise above the fog and the clouds, everything is bright and clear; the sun is shining, and you can look down on the gloom below. This illustration is a lesson for us that, with God's help, we, too, can rise above our troubles when we pay attention to God's Word where we can see things from God's perspective.

Verse 51: "The proud have had me greatly in derision: yet have I not declined from thy law" (KJV).

The psalmist expressed his feelings toward the people who were ungodly, full of pride and who did not believe in God. These people scoffed at him and were arrogant towards him. The psalmist, like most of us, was affected by what people were doing and saying to him; his faith was being shaken. But even in these circumstances he never morally deflected from the law, which is God's moral standard that is made clear for us in the Bible. Men and women can be cruel. Men and women can be hurtful and can attack a Christian in different ways. How do you deflect this? How do you stand fast in these attacks? You again need to turn to your Bible and read how Jesus was hated and rejected by mankind when He lived in this world. So it is not at all surprising that as a follower of Jesus you can expect the same treatment. In Ephesians 6:16, we are encouraged to put on the shield of faith which deflects the darts of the wicked. So, by reading the Bible we get encouragement to stand against the evil attacks for the sake of our Lord and Saviour Jesus Christ.

Verse 52: "I remembered thy judgments of old, O LORD; and have comforted myself" (KJV).

The psalmist casts his mind back to the way that God had come in mighty judgment and power upon the ungodly who discarded His name and did evil against His people Israel. The psalmist may have thought about the time when the Israelites were fleeing from captivity in Egypt (see Exodus 14:1-31). The Egyptians were chasing them, and the people were afraid (verse 10). But God opened the Red Sea to allow His people to cross on dry land (verses 21-22) and, when they were safely over to the other side, He brought the water back down on all the Egyptians (verse 23). Or maybe the psalmist was thinking back to the tower of Babel when mankind wanted to make a name for themselves and tried to build a tower that would reach Heaven (Genesis 11:1-9). The LORD came down and made the people speak different languages so they could not understand each other and scattered them all over the earth. It is clear in the Bible that, when the time is right, God deals with the one who scoffs. Psalm 2:4 tells us that the LORD will laugh at the scoffers. The LORD is taking note of those who are going against Him and against His people. The psalmist found great comfort as he took the scrolls and read of God's dealings with men in judgment. Dear fellow believer, if someone is hurting you in this way, be sure they are hurting your Lord and that He, the judge of all the earth, will do right! (See Genesis 18:25). Dig into your Bible and find encouragement and comfort as the psalmist did.

Verse 53: "Horror hath taken hold upon me because of the wicked that forsake thy law" (KJV).

The psalmist shows his compassion for those around him. They have no desire for the things of the Lord and some even go as far as to scoff at God and the people of God. Every true believer in Christ should have compassion toward our neighbours, our friends, our family, the people we work with, and those we rub shoulders with daily in our streets. Every person who forsakes God's law and rejects God's offer of salvation through faith in His son Jesus Christ is heading for the final judgment day and eternal damnation. We know this; the Bible makes it very clear! Therefore, like the psalmist, we should have a real zeal to preach the Gospel of the saving grace of our Lord Jesus Christ.

> "[God] will have all men to be saved, and
> to come unto the knowledge of the truth"
> (1 Timothy 2:4, KJV).

This would teach us that we should feel pity for even those who scoff at us or make things difficult for us. We need to pray for them, have compassion on them and desire to have the opportunity to win them for Christ. Being able to do this takes grace and humility and sometimes swallowing our own pride and feelings. But again our help and example is found in the Bible as we read of our wonderful Saviour who washed the feet of Judas, whom the Lord knew was about to betray Him (see John 13:1-30).

Verse 54: "Thy statutes have been my songs in the house of my pilgrimage" (KJV).

The psalmist speaks of what keeps him singing during his life, even during times of affliction. The songs he sang came from the Word of God because he was obedient to it and was cheered by it. What do you sing about? Do your songs come from your heart and give thanks and praise to God? Maybe you have a problem singing, not because you are a bad singer but because you do not have the joy in your heart that causes you to sing. Maybe you feel detached from God because of your way of life, and you struggle to sing. Dear reader, there is nothing like confessing your sin and renewing that relationship with your God and Saviour. The "house" speaks of our body and "pilgrimage" would speak of the life we live on earth. A statute means a divine direction to obtain our obedience; there is great joy for us when we are obedient to the Word of God:

> "And He hath put a new song in my mouth, even praise unto our God: many shall see it, and fear, and shall trust in the LORD" (Psalm 40:3, KJV).

Our lives as Christians can speak volumes to others. As we read the Bible, there are many things in it that should make our hearts sing.

Verse 55: "I have remembered thy name, O LORD, in the night, and have kept thy law" (KJV).

Here is the third mention of the word "remember":

1. Verse 49: "*Remember* the word unto thy servant."
2. Verse 52: "I *remembered* thy judgments of old."
3. Verse 55: "I have *remembered* thy name, O LORD."

Perhaps verse 55 is the most precious of all three. In Malachi 3:16 we read about the faithful remnant, who feared the LORD, and that thought upon His name. His name meant everything to them; the LORD knew it and He appreciated it. How much does the name of Jesus mean to you? In Matthew 18:20 Jesus said: "Where two or three are gathered together in my name, there am I in the midst of them." Both these verses should encourage us. Many of us gather together in church in small numbers to remember the Lord, but oh what joy we have when we come together in His Name and claim His promise that He is with us! There is also joy for the Lord as He hears our thanksgiving and prayers.

The "night" in the Bible sometimes speaks of a time of terror, trouble, tears, temptation, and tragedy. Often if something or someone is troubling you, you become anxious during the night, you cannot sleep, your mind is racing, your feel agitated and you are struggling to be at peace. The psalmist had troubles and his way of peace was that he remembered his LORD in the night. He could think about the LORD because he had been faithful to the law of God, or for you and me today, the Bible. There was no sin in his life that would keep him from enjoying thoughts about the LORD. His heart was right, and he could meditate upon the LORD and be happy and be at peace as he remembered all the many precious promises the LORD had made.

What are your thoughts as you lay your head on your pillow or as you waken during the night? It would be wonderful if your thoughts were always drawn to the Name of our Lord. Another way of looking at this is that sometimes our spiritual experience is comparable to the night when things are dark; we are restless and long for the morning to dawn.

Verse 56: "This I had, because I kept thy precepts" (KJV).

With these words, the psalmist ends this stanza. The Amplified Bible renders verse 56:

> "This I have had [as the gift of Your grace and as my reward]: that I have kept Your precepts [hearing, receiving, loving, and obeying them]" (AB).

The first time I read this, I thought that the psalmist was speaking of the experience he previously enjoyed because now he was not in the good of these things. But, after careful study, I think he was acknowledging the Lord's grace in his life and one reason for this was that he was continuing in obedience to the Word of God.

Conclusion

This stanza we have studied underlines the importance of reading and studying the Bible, which is the Word of God. We have been reminded that the Bible brings hope, comfort, life, singing and peace. But to have the daily enjoyment of these things, we must be obedient to the Word of God. God demands it. The Bible is the handbook for life, and it is our sword, part of the armour of God, which we must put on daily (see Ephesians 6:10-18).

ה

## 8.	CHETH – verses 57-64

George E Stevens

Introduction

The structure of Psalm 119 has been explained in the Introduction to this book. The number eight is significant to this stanza, CHETH, because CHETH is also the eighth letter of the Hebrew alphabet. In the Scriptures, the number "8" denotes a "new beginning" or "resurrection". For example, Noah, who stepped out onto a regenerated earth, is called "the eighth person" in 2 Peter 2:5 and, of the earth's population at the time, only eight souls were saved. Furthermore, we can find eight resurrections of specific individuals in the Scriptures other than that of Christ Himself. In fact, if we look at the mathematical total of the numbers represented by the Greek letters that spell "Jesus", we find 888. He is the Resurrection and the Life! There is no one to compare with Him relative to new beginnings.

Verse 57a: "Thou art my portion, O Lord" (KJV).

CHETH means a "portion" or "share", hence, the literal translation: "My portion".

In Psalm 16:5-6 we read words of David written in the spirit of Christ:

> "The Lord is the portion of mine inheritance and of my cup: thou maintainest my lot. The lines are fallen unto me in pleasant places; yea, I have a goodly heritage" (KJV).

These verses show that the word "portion" parallels the idea of an inheritance. This is supported by Deuteronomy 10:9:

> "Wherefore Levi hath no part nor inheritance with his brethren; the Lord is his inheritance, according as the Lord thy God promised him" (KJV).

Psalm 142:5 also strengthens the thought:

> "I cried unto thee, O Lord: I said, Thou art my refuge and my portion in the land of the living" (KJV).

But what is the force of saying, "The Lord is my portion"? On the one hand, it tells us that the psalmist placed the Lord above everything else.

In 1 Samuel 2:2 we find Hannah stating in her prayer:

> "There is none holy as the Lord: for there is none beside thee: neither is there any rock like our God" (KJV).

David could also say:

> "Among the gods there is none like unto thee, O Lord; neither are there any works like unto thy works" (Psalm 86:8, KJV).

Jeremiah also knew this truth:

> "Forasmuch as there is none like unto thee, O LORD; thou art great, and thy name is great in might" (Jeremiah 10:6, KJV).

Our God is almighty, immortal, all-knowing, unchanging, ever-present, light, life, and love. He is ever faithful and ever true. Every resource in heaven and earth are at His disposal. What a realisation that the LORD is my portion!

In the words of the Apostle Paul:

> "If God be for us, who can be against us?" (Romans 8:31, KJV).

On the other hand, the wonder of His Person demands our submission to His will and purposes. The LORD said to Abram:

> "Get thee out of thy country, and from thy kindred, and from thy father's house, unto a land that I will shew thee" (Genesis 12:1, KJV).

This meant a huge upheaval for Abram, but in faith he trusted and obeyed.

Verse 57b: "I have said that I would keep thy words" (KJV).

Like Abram, the psalmist is committed to keep the Word of the LORD. Why? Not only because of the greatness of

God's person, but because the psalmist loved Him. The Lord Jesus said:

> "If a man love me, he will keep my words: and my Father will love him, and we will come unto him, and make our abode with him" (John 14:23, KJV).

It is well said that the measure of love for God is obedience. The "words" mentioned in John 14:23 encompass all that the Saviour said. They include both His sayings and His commandments. It is sometimes said that:

- To keep the commands of Jesus is the duty of love.
- To keep His sayings is the life of love.
- To keep His words is the joy of love.

Of course, the Word of the Lord is tempered with light and love. It always seeks the best for His children. We could say that by obeying His Word, we are dwelling in His love.

Verse 58a: "I intreated thy favour with my whole heart" (KJV).

The psalmist makes a strong statement for the word "intreated" has the force of "rubbing" or "wearing out". We could say that the psalmist had worn out the favour of God with persistent prayer from a sincere and affectionate heart. He knew the overflowing grace of His God and tapped into it with his supplications. In Luke 18:2-8, we find an example of this attitude for prayer. There, the Lord Jesus spoke of a widow who pursued her case against an adversary with an unbelieving judge. The latter would not take up her case; but the widow persisted with her plea. Finally, the judge gave in saying within himself:

> "Though I fear not God, nor regard man;
> yet because this widow troubleth me, I
> will avenge her, lest by her continual
> coming she weary me" (Luke 18:4-5,
> KJV).

That is the sort of prayer in which the psalmist engaged and how much faster the LORD would have responded!

Verse 58b: "Be merciful unto me according to Thy word" (KJV).

The psalmist follows on from verse 58a with this immediate request. The Hebrew meaning of the word for "merciful" has the force of one stooping in kindness to an inferior. David makes a similar request:

> "Have mercy upon me, O God, according
> to thy lovingkindness: according unto the
> multitude of thy tender mercies blot out
> my transgressions" (Psalm 51:1, KJV).

David had sinned grievously (see 2 Samuel 11:1-12:15) and was seeking the same mercy from God in order to be forgiven. He reminds God of the kindness of His nature and the abundance of His compassion. In Psalm 119, the psalmist reminds God that His Word says that He is kind and, therefore, to uphold the truth of His Word, He must act accordingly. This praying saint uses God's own Word as a lever to move His arm in mercy.

Verse 59a: "I thought on my ways" (KJV).

The psalmist had considered his ways and, without doubt, the motives that moved him. He decided which were right and which were wrong. He thought of the consequences that resulted from them. He wondered which of them brought glory to God. An example of this kind of thinking is where the LORD asks the people of Judah to consider their ways:

> "Consider your ways. Ye have sown much, and bring in little; ye eat, but ye have not enough; ye drink, but ye are not filled with drink; ye clothe you, but there is none warm; and he that earneth wages earneth wages to put it into a bag with holes" (Haggai 1:5-6, KJV).

Their sinful ways had made any blessing void. In contrast, we find in Psalm 128:1-2:

> "Blessed is every one that feareth the LORD; that walketh in his ways. For thou shalt eat the labour of thine hands: happy shalt thou be, and it shall be well with thee" (KJV).

What are His ways like? Psalm 145:17 has the answer – they are righteous. The first part of Proverbs 11:5 shows that our righteousness will direct our way. Of course, the cleansing of our way is the result of obedience to God's Word (Psalm 119:9). Hence, we have the next part of the psalmist's sentence.

Verse 59b: "And turned my feet unto thy testimonies" (KJV).

Testimonies are the proven truths concerning the attributes, ways and works of God, especially those presented in the Law of Moses. The Psalmist turned away from his old ways to walk in complete obedience to the will of God as found in the Scriptures. This would have included repentance, which is a change of mind that, over time, results in a pure heart.

Verse 60: "I made haste, and delayed not to keep thy commandments" (KJV).

The word used for "haste" means to be "eager with excitement or joy". This is emphasised by the clause: "I delayed not...", which shows the immediate response of the psalmist to keep the commandments of the LORD. There was no questioning or reluctance at all. This was the attitude of the Lord Jesus Christ as the Perfect Servant on earth. He was obedient unto death, even the death of the cross (see Philippians 2:8). He said:

> "Lo, I come (in the volume of the book it
> is written of me,) to do thy will, O God"
> (Hebrews 10:7, KJV).

We have a saying, "Procrastination is the thief of time!" Every hour we lose in not obeying the Lord reduces our investment in Glory where the treasures of our faith are being stored. Will we receive a commendation for faithfulness from the Lord when we arrive in the harbour of heaven or will we drift to our destination in a state of shipwreck? The procrastinating servant is characterised by the following poem:

> "To-morrow," he said to his spirit,
> "Tomorrow, the Lord I'll believe.
> Tomorrow, I'll pray as I ought to
> Tomorrow, to God, I will cleave.
> Tomorrow, I'll walk by His Spirit
> And for Him good fruit I shall bear.
> Tomorrow, I'll worship and witness
> And show to all others I care."

"Tomorrow, I'll serve with rejoicing,
Working by night and by day."
"Tomorrow!" he said with conviction,
"The Lord God shall show me His way.
Tomorrow, my zeal shall be witnessed.
Tomorrow, I'll set time aside.
Tomorrow, my all, I shall give Him.
Know that He stays by my side."

The marching of time was relentless;
"Tomorrow" had nothing to gain;
For, as life's short journey was ending,
His body was weakened by pain.
Tomorrow had never delivered
An item of joy for the Lord.
No treasure was stored in the heavens
And lost was the Saviour's reward.

The Apostle Paul exhorts:

> "See then that ye walk circumspectly, not
> as fools, but as wise, redeeming the time,
> because the days are evil" (Ephesians
> 5:15-16, KJV).

There is a great deal of glitter in this world which seeks to captivate our hearts; but the Word of the Lord tells us to buy back the time so that we may faithfully and earnestly serve God.

Verse 61: "The bands of the wicked have robbed me: but I have not forgotten thy law" (KJV).

This verse shows us that the psalmist had enemies who had bound him with cords. As Young's Literal Translation puts it:

> "Cords of the wicked have surrounded
> me..." (YLT).

This suggests that even when held as a prisoner, he had not forgotten the law of God. His body may have been bound, but his faith was free. The Apostle Paul is a good example of this. Though chained to guards in prison, he was still allowed to write. The result was what are called "Prison Epistles", which include: Ephesians, Philippians, Colossians, and Philemon.

We have three enemies who seek to bind us: the World, the Flesh, and the Devil.

> "Love not the world, neither the things that are in the world. If any man love the world, the love of the Father is not in him. For all that is in the world, the lust of the flesh, and the lust of the eyes, and the pride of life, is not of the Father, but is of the world. And the world passeth away, and the lust thereof: but he that doeth the will of God abideth for ever" (1 John 2:15-17, KJV).

The world is that system of things formed by mankind's thoughts and activities that opposes the will of God. It is by the power of the cross alone that the world is crucified to the believer, and the believer to the world (see Galatians 6:14).

The flesh is that sinful nature, inherent in natural man, which constantly seeks self-exaltation, self-gratification, and self-satisfaction. The Christian is to flee from the strong desires of his self-centred nature. He is to recognise that his old nature has been crucified with Christ:

> "I am crucified with Christ: nevertheless I live; yet not I, but Christ liveth in me: and

the life which I now live in the flesh I live
by the faith of the Son of God, who
loved me, and gave himself for me"
(Galatians 2:20, KJV, but see also
Galatians 5:24).

The Christian should live by the righteous nature that
God gave to him when he first believed.

The devil seeks to destroy faith in God. The world is but
one of the tools he uses to do this. He is both the god and
prince of this world (2 Corinthians 4:4; John 12:31). A
Christian is to resist him and to avoid the snares he sets
for him (James 4:7).

Verse 62: "At midnight I will rise to give thanks unto thee because of thy righteous judgments" (KJV).

Here is a remarkable act of devotion. The psalmist
purposely rose from bed at midnight in order to praise
and worship the LORD. At night, when we pray beside our
beds, tiredness often spoils our concentration and, at
times, we find it difficult to stay awake. The LORD's
judgments, which are both true and just (Psalm 19:9),
brought so much respect and joy to the psalmist following
his meditations that he was prepared to diligently praise
the Lord in the middle of the night. In Acts 16:25 we read
of the Apostle Paul and Silas (in prison) praying and
singing praises to God even though they had suffered
physical abuse previously.

Verse 63: "I am a companion of all them that fear thee, and of them that keep thy precepts" (KJV).

We have a proverb that says, "Birds of a feather flock
together." This means that people of like mind, tastes and

interests will be found together. So, anyone who has trusted in God will ensure that he meets with fellow believers. In 2 Timothy 2:22 we are exhorted:

> "…follow righteousness, faith, charity, peace, with them that call on the Lord out of a pure heart" (KJV).

Today, faithful Christians meet and serve the Lord together. They prefer the prayer meeting to the pub; and the Bible study to the dance. They regularly speak of God and spiritual things one to the other (Malachi 3:16).

Verse 64: "The earth, O LORD, is full of thy mercy: teach me thy statutes" (KJV).

The word for "mercy" is "kindness". It covers the fact that God does not judge us in the way we deserve. His kindness seeks to bless us. This kindness defends us, provides for us, encourages us, assures us, comforts us, and heals us. As the prophet Jeremiah has said:

> "It is of the LORD's mercies that we are not consumed, because his compassions fail not. They are new every morning: great is thy faithfulness. The LORD is my portion, saith my soul; therefore will I hope in him" (Lamentations 3:22-24, KJV).

Lamentations 3:24 take us back to where we started in Psalm 119:57.

Conclusion

I summarise this meditation with a poem:

> You are my portion, gracious Lord,
> The portion that I chose.
> I am resolved Your word to keep
> For it Your person shows.
>
> Your face, I seek with all my heart
> For with Your grace it gleams.
> According to Your precious word
> Your mercy to me beams.
>
> My life was foolish and perverse!
> Dark sin had filled my days;
> But testimonies wise and true
> Turned me from wicked ways.
>
> Most hastily Your laws I'll keep;
> My heart with You I'll share.
> I shall not dwell in slothfulness;
> But Your reproach shall bear.
>
> Though cords of wicked men restrain
> The body that I wear.
> My faith shall be at liberty;
> To Your precepts repair.
>
> At midnight, I shall bless Your name
> For judgments just and true.
> I'll gather with the faithful, Lord,
> All those who trust in You.
>
> O Lord, Your mercy e'er endures;
> It fully fills the earth.
> Oh, teach me all I need to know
> As I explore Your worth.

ט

9.　TETH – verses 65-72

Stephen Thomson

Verse 65: "Thou hast dealt well with thy servant, O Lord, according unto thy word" (KJV).

In this statement, I believe the psalmist was happily acknowledging God's goodness in His dealings with mankind. "Thy word"[14] has a similar meaning to the Greek word *"logos"* and it means the articulation of God's will to men. Just as Peter speaks of "the oracles of God" (1 Peter 4:11). "Thy word" is first used in verse 9:

> "Wherewithal shall a young man cleanse
> his way? by taking heed thereto according
> to thy word" (KJV).

It is also used in verse 89:

> "For ever, O Lord, thy word is settled in
> heaven" (KJV).

[14] There are two different Hebrew words translated by the English word "word" in verses 65 and 67. They occur almost in equal numbers throughout Psalm 119.

The psalmist is thinking of the greatness of God and bows down before Him as His servant. Many a master would deal unkindly and perhaps even cruelly with his servant, but not the LORD. David could say:

> "The LORD is merciful and gracious, slow to anger, and plenteous in mercy" (Psalm 103:8, KJV).

If we have come to know the Lord Jesus Christ as our Saviour and Lord, then we have special cause to thank God for His goodness. The Apostle Paul tells us that it is "the goodness of God which leads men to repentance" (Romans 2:4). It is certainly true that, if we have a deep sense in our souls of the goodness of God, it will help us face the trials of life and any adversity which comes our way.

Verse 66: "Teach me good judgment and knowledge: for I have believed thy commandments" (KJV).

Not for the first time the psalmist prays, "Teach me", which he repeats in verse 68. Thus, there are 8 other times (in the King James Version), when he prays this prayer "Teach me" in this psalm:

1. "Blessed art thou, O LORD: *teach* me thy statutes" (verse 12).

2. "I have declared my ways, and thou heardest me: *teach* me thy statutes" (verse 26).

3. "*Teach* me, O LORD, the way of thy statutes; and I shall keep it unto the end" (verse 33).

4. "The earth, O LORD, is full of thy mercy: *teach* me thy statutes" (verse 64).

5. "Thou art good, and doest good; *teach* me thy statutes" (verse 68).

6. "Accept, I beseech thee, the freewill offerings of my mouth, O LORD, and *teach* me thy judgments" (verse 108). "Thy judgments" – the thought is a sentence of a judge.

7. "Deal with thy servant according unto thy mercy, and *teach* me thy statutes" (verse 124).

8. "Make thy face to shine upon thy servant; and *teach* me thy statutes" (verse 135).

When I was younger, I had a desire to learn the accordion. My father found someone who was willing to teach me, but alas, I think I was un-teachable! My teacher was a good player and put time and effort into teaching me, but I did not do the work. I wanted to play football with my friends rather than practise my music. I wonder, are we teachable in the things of God, in His will for our lives?

The people of God in the Old Testament had the Law of Moses, and "Thy commandments" (verse 66) has the thought of both commands and prohibitions. But in the perfect life of the Lord Jesus Christ, lived in this world, as recorded in the Gospels, and in the apostles' doctrine, as taught in the epistles, we see fully the requirements of God's will for us. The question is, are we willing and prepared to be taught? You will notice that the psalmist prays for "good judgment and knowledge" (verse 66). Wisdom and knowledge are not necessarily the same. Knowledge is important, we need it, but wisdom informs us how to act with that knowledge. It has been well said, "Knowledge is knowing that a tomato is a fruit; wisdom is not putting it in a fruit salad." In succeeding king David, Solomon asked God for wisdom (see 1 Kings 3). In our modern day there seem to be limitless sources of knowledge, but at the same time a lack of wisdom shown by many. Of course, I am writing of godly wisdom – not the wisdom of men, which Paul dismisses as foolishness:

> "For the preaching of the cross is to them that perish foolishness; but unto us which are saved it is the power of God. For it is written, I will destroy the wisdom of the wise, and will bring to nothing the understanding of the prudent. Where is the wise? where is the scribe? where is the disputer of this world? hath not God made foolish the wisdom of this world? For after that in the wisdom of God the world by wisdom knew not God, it pleased God by the foolishness of preaching to save them that believe. For the Jews require a sign, and the Greeks seek after wisdom: But we preach Christ crucified, unto the Jews a stumblingblock, and unto the Greeks foolishness; But unto them which are called, both Jews and Greeks, Christ the power of God, and the wisdom of God. Because the foolishness of God is wiser than men; and the weakness of God is stronger than men" (1 Corinthians 1:18-25, KJV).

We need to prayerfully seek the wisdom of God:

> "If any of you lack wisdom, let him ask of God, that giveth to all men liberally, and upbraideth not; and it shall be given him" (James 1:5, KJV).

Verse 67: "Before I was afflicted I went astray: but now have I kept thy word" (KJV).

We have no idea what sorrowful experience the psalmist had passed through, but it would appear that he recognised that this experience was for his ultimate good. I know it is becoming less accepted in our society today, but discipline is an act of love. The Bible teaches this. We read in the book of Proverbs:

> "My son, despise not the chastening of the LORD; neither be weary of his correction: for whom the LORD loveth he correcteth; even as a father the son in whom he delighteth" (Proverbs 3:11-12, KJV).

The writer to the Hebrews quotes these words and adds:

> "Now no chastening for the present seemeth to be joyous, but grievous: nevertheless afterward it yieldeth the peaceable fruit of righteousness unto them which are exercised thereby" (Hebrews 12:11, KJV).

However, I do not want to give the impression that any, or every, trial we pass through is necessarily God's chastisement upon us for our waywardness. That is where Job's comforters (so called) went wrong, in their assumption that Job must have sinned to be in the situation he was in. But it does us good to remember that our Father's hand is always upon us, for blessing and good, even if it takes His chastening to bring it about in our lives.

The word used for "thy word" in verse 67 has the meaning of "a saying". It could be a poetic word or speech, or sacred hymn but communicated orally. It does appear that the psalmist recognised that he had been disobedient in relation to God's sayings, His Word.

Verse 68: "Thou art good, and doest good; teach me thy statutes" (KJV).

Again the psalmist returns to the theme of God's goodness and prays to be taught. God is good, and He does good! When God answers our prayers, and heals us or helps us in some way, we readily say, "God is good." But the challenge for us is to recognise that even when things do not work out as we had hoped and prayed, God is still good! I remember speaking with a young man after he had just sung a solo at the funeral service of his stepmother. I said how remarkable I thought it was that he could sing this hymn of praise on such an occasion. His reply was, "We praise God on the good days, and we praise Him on the bad days too." He is right, of course, and what a challenge that is! Perhaps with the Apostle Paul we can say:

> "And we know that all things work together for good to them that love God…" (Romans 8:28, KJV).

Remember, too, the words of Job:

> "The LORD gave, and the LORD hath taken away; blessed be the name of the LORD" (Job 1:21, KJV).

Job did not only recognise the hand of God in his difficult circumstances, but he also acknowledged His providence with him, and he blessed the name of the LORD. What a man of faith he was!

The word used for "thy statutes", in "Teach me thy statutes", has the thought of a mark carved or engraved, a definite limit set. In New Testament language, the psalmist wanted to keep himself in the love of God. He wanted to be approved of God, by being obedient to His Word.

Verse 69: "The proud have forged a lie against me: but I will keep thy precepts with my whole heart" (KJV).

Pride is a dreadful thing and is even spoken of by non-Christians in a negative way. If we are true followers of the Lord Jesus, let us seek to be humble, following in His steps (see 1 Peter 2:21). From Psalm 119:51, we know that these proud people had derided the psalmist. They had mocked him mercilessly, although we are not told the reason why. We read that they forged a lie against him. To me, the idea of forging is one of effort and requires work, which suggests that these people had worked hard to make this lie against him. You will remember Daniel and how those who sought to bring him down could not find fault in him (Daniel 6:1-4). So they had to forge, to manufacture, a situation where his praying to his God was against the king's commandment (Daniel 6:5-23). Not too long afterwards, they met with a terrible end (Daniel 6:24), as will all who are proud and liars, if they do not repent. We may experience this too, lies being told against us, and men mocking us. The Lord Jesus told His disciples, as He prepared them for His departure out of this world:

"If the world hate you, ye know that it hated me before it hated you" (see John 15:18, KJV).

Sometimes, the trouble is that the things people say about us, mocking us, may well be true. How we need to remember God's precepts!

The word used for "thy precepts" has the thought of a charge given to us by God for which we are responsible. Peter's words are worth noting:

> "But let none of you suffer as a murderer, or as a thief, or as an evildoer, or as a busybody in other men's matters. Yet if any man suffer as a Christian, let him not be ashamed; but let him glorify God on this behalf" (1 Peter 4:15-16, KJV).

Verse 70: "Their heart is as fat as grease; but I delight in thy law" (KJV).

This verse is linked with the previous one and is the psalmist's view of those proud and lying persons. I do not know what you make of the statement, "Their heart is as fat as grease", but it certainly is not a complimentary one! I am sure this is not a reference to their physical appearance but rather to their spiritual condition. (I say spiritual as man is a spiritual being, not that these people have spiritual life). As far as I know, this is the only time this word translated "fat" is used in the Scriptures, so we are unable to compare Scripture with Scripture. However, sometimes the thought of fatness in the Scriptures is a very positive thing. Recently a brother in Christ wrote to me, thanking me for doing a service for him, and quoted, "the soul of the diligent shall be made fat" (see Proverbs

13:4). I was slightly bemused, but I took it as a compliment. But there was nothing complimentary about the words the psalmist writes about these people.

In contrast to these proud and spiritually lifeless people, the psalmist could say that he delighted in the law of the LORD. The word used for "the law of the LORD" has the thought of teaching or instruction. It is good if we have the energy of heart to be able to be taught and instructed in the Word of God.

Verse 71: "It is good for me that I have been afflicted; that I might learn thy statutes" (KJV).

In verse 67, the psalmist recognised that the affliction which had come upon him was for his good, because it resulted in him keeping the Word of the LORD. Perhaps he did not appreciate this at the time but looking back over the years he had come to see the value in the trials he had passed through. Perhaps you know the anonymous poem:

> Not until the loom is silent,
> And the shuttles cease to fly,
> Will God unroll the pattern
> And explain the reason why.
>
> The dark threads are as needful
> In the weaver's skilful hand,
> As the threads of gold and silver
> For the pattern which He planned.

Again, "thy statutes" is used by the psalmist – the word has the thought of a mark carved or engraved as a definite limit set. The psalmist had learnt these boundaries through the experience of affliction. It may be that we are passed through difficult experiences so that we also may learn lessons in the school of God.

Verse 72: "The law of thy mouth is better unto me than thousands of gold and silver."

Often men misquote the Scripture and say, "Money is the root of all evil". But the Apostle Paul did not say that! He said:

> "*The love of* money is a root of all evil" (1 Timothy 6:10).

Today we hear people speaking of millions, billions and even trillions, but in Old Testament times, 'thousands' was the biggest number in common use. Here in the last verse of this stanza, verse 72, the psalmist is saying in effect, that the teaching and instruction of the LORD, is better than millions, billions or even trillions of gold and silver. The word "better" is only found this once in Psalm 119, although the words "well" (verse 65), and "good" (verses 68 and 71) have the same root. In the King James Version, the word "better" is used a total of seven times in The Book of Psalms – here in verse 72 and:

1. "A little that a righteous man hath is *better* than the riches of many wicked" (37:16).

2. "Because thy lovingkindness is *better* than life, my lips shall praise thee" (63:3).

3. "This also shall please the LORD *better* than an ox or bullock that hath horns and hoofs" (69:31).

4. "For a day in thy courts is *better* than a thousand. I had rather be a doorkeeper in the house of my God, than to dwell in the tents of wickedness" (84:10).

5. "It is *better* to trust in the LORD than to put confidence in man" (118:8).

6. "It is *better* to trust in the LORD than to put confidence in princes" (118:9).

ר

10.   YOD – verses 73-80

Ian D Britton

Introduction

"To be a Christian without prayer is no more possible
than to be alive without breathing." So wrote Martin
Luther sometime in the sixteenth century. It remains true
today. The people of God have always needed to
communicate with Him by prayer, and we can learn a
great deal from the many prayers recorded in the Bible.
After the first three verses of Psalm 119, the whole text
is addressed directly to God. We can therefore consider
this stanza, and nearly all the rest of the psalm, to be a
prayer, making it, arguably, the longest prayer recorded in
God's Word. As we read it and work through its meaning,
we need to consider whether we could, or should, pray to
God along similar lines in our day.

Verses 73-80 are the tenth stanza of this poem, and each
of these eight verses in Hebrew commences with the
letter YOD. This derives from the Hebrew word YAD
meaning hand. There is an obvious reference to this

meaning in verse 73: "Your hands have made me." We might think of verses such as:

- "In the shadow of His *hand* He has hidden me" (Isaiah 49:2).

- "The good *hand* of his God [was] upon [Ezra], for [he] had prepared his heart to seek the law of the LORD and to do it" (Ezra 7:9-10).

- "Therefore humble yourselves under the mighty *hand* of God, that He may exalt you in due time" (1 Peter 5:6).

We will certainly see the hand of God on the psalmist's life as we work through each verse of this stanza.

Verse 73: "Your hands have made me and fashioned me; give me understanding, that I may learn Your commandments."

GOD KNOWS ME!

God knows me inside and out because He made me. He knows all about mankind as a whole because He is our Creator. He knows all about me as an individual because it is God who gave me life and formed me before I was even born. He therefore knows all my weaknesses and strengths; physical, mental, and emotional. God knows my "drivers" and the things with which I struggle and am apt to fail. Since my birth, He has overseen the whole of my experience and circumstances until now, and so knows everything that has shaped my thinking and reactions. He knows why I do what I do, both good and bad. All of this means that the Lord knows perfectly what is best for me at every level. This appreciation gave confidence to the psalmist to pray that God might give him understanding, and it should give us the same confidence.

Our Father knows what we are capable of understanding. He knows the best ways for us to learn and how to move us and keep us on a new course. We often want more understanding: about the world, about our lives, about the future, even about the Bible. But do we want to learn God's commandments with a view to obeying them? Notice it is the commandments, things to do, or not do, that the psalmist wants to understand. We know from the rest of this psalm that the writer is always interested in knowing more of God's commandments for two principal reasons:

- So that he can do them.
- So that he can know God better.

Mere intellectual curiosity about God's Word, or the ability to win arguments and debates with other believers, or a desire to reinforce what we already know we want to do, are never good reasons to study God's Word, and we cannot expect prayers with such motives to be answered.

Verse 74: "Those who fear You will be glad when they see me, because I have hoped in Your word."

OTHERS SEE ME!

Are you being a help and an encouragement to other believers? The New Testament has some great examples for us:

Philemon lifted the spirits of his fellow Christians:

> "The hearts of the saints have been refreshed by you, brother" (Philemon 1:7).

Seeing how Paul was strengthened by God in his difficulties encouraged others to follow his example:

"Most of the brethren in the Lord, having become confident by my chains, are much more bold to speak the word without fear" (Philippians 1:14).

Epaphroditus was worthy of honour and imitation in his service for Christ:

"Receive him therefore in the Lord with all gladness, and hold such men in esteem; because for the work of Christ he came close to death" (Philippians 2:29-30).

What impact do we have on other Christians when they look at us? Some Christians only have to walk into a room to be an encouragement and an uplifting influence. Others can quench the joy of a whole company by their presence. Which kind of believer am I?

The meaning of the psalmist in verse 74 is that others would look at him, remember that he had hoped in the Lord and not been disappointed, and receive encouragement to trust, or continue trusting, themselves. The others were being directed towards God rather than the psalmist. They saw the writer, recognised that his God was trustworthy, and therefore followed his good example of faith. Is that not what we should all aspire to do for other people? It reminds me of a verse from a hymn by Kate B Wilkinson (1859 – 1928):

May His beauty rest upon me
As I seek the lost to win,
And may they forget the channel,
Seeing only Him.

Where is our hope placed? Is it firmly in God and His Word? We cannot aspire to point others towards God if all our hopes are based firmly in this world.

Verse 75: "I know, O LORD, that Your judgments are right, and that in faithfulness You have afflicted me."

GOD IS RIGHT!

Verse 75 sets out an important, basic principle: God is right whatever may have happened!

The writer is looking at first causes, and is able to say, "You have afflicted me." Now he could probably have phrased it as "the wicked have afflicted me", or "Satan has afflicted me", or just, "bad stuff happens"! But, instead, he looks right through all those secondary causes and recognises that God is directing everything, and the affliction therefore comes from Him. Judging from verse 76, it seems that the psalmist had done something wrong, and he acknowledges that God's response is both reasonable and deserved. Are we also ready to acknowledge that God is always right, whatever He may send into our lives? Not only does the psalmist accept that the affliction is fair, he also considers it to be "faithful". It is a part of the Father's faithfulness to us that we are corrected and admonished:

> "Whom the LORD loves He chastens.
> ...If you endure chastening, God deals
> with you as sons" (Hebrews 12:6-7).

I have been reading through the book of Proverbs recently and it has a great deal to say about the right and wrong ways to handle chastening:

- "A scoffer does not listen to rebuke" (13:1).

- "Poverty and shame will come to him who disdains correction" (13:18).

- "A fool despises his father's instruction, but he who receives correction is prudent" (15:5).

And there are many more! The wise respond positively to affliction and correction; those who reject it are fools!

Verse 76: "Let, I pray, Your merciful kindness be for my comfort, according to Your word to Your servant."

GOD COMFORTS US!

When we have been afflicted and have responded correctly with humility, contrition, and a readiness to learn from the experience, we need to be comforted. A child who has received a telling off from mum or dad, once contrite, will come back for a hug, and to be reassured that mum and dad still love him!

Kindness is a much-underrated virtue! It is a characteristic of God, and one that we ought to copy. Kindness is one part of the fruit of the Spirit described in Galatians 5:22-23. According to Romans 2:4, the kindness of God is meant to lead people to repentance. It consists of acting generously towards people even when they do not deserve it, just like God did towards us before we repented. In verse 76 God's merciful kindness produces comfort. Paul describes God as:

> "The Father of mercies and God of all comfort, Who comforts us in all our tribulation, that we may be able to comfort those who are in any trouble, with the comfort with which we ourselves are comforted by God" (2 Corinthians 1:3-4).

So the comfort that God brings to us, through his mercy and kindness, is to be shared with others who are in any trouble.

With the phrase "according to Your word to Your servant" (verse 76b), the psalmist reminds God of His promises. This is very much a scriptural type of prayer, to base our requests on what God Himself has already promised. The writer reminds God that he is God's own servant, that is, he belongs to Him, and is His to direct and protect.

Verse 77: "Let Your tender mercies come to me, that I may live; for Your law is my delight."

GOD IS TENDER!

God does not just show mercy, He has "*tender* mercies" (verse 77). God always has them; the psalmist just needs them to come to him. The tenderness of God is a beautiful thing, and all the more remarkable given His greatness and power. We do not often associate tenderness with the mighty and powerful, but God has the tender care of a mother for her vulnerable child.

We are truly totally dependent on God. We cannot live without Him. This is true, physically:

God is the only Sustainer of the universe:

> "In Him all things consist" (Colossians 1:17).

He holds our breath in His hand:

> "In Whose hand is the life of every living thing, and the breath of all mankind?" (Job 12:10).

It is also true of our life of faith – we need the Lord to keep us and maintain us:

- "You will keep him in perfect peace, whose mind is stayed on You, because he trusts in You" (Isaiah 26:3).

- "The life which I now live in the flesh I live by faith in the Son of God, Who loved me, and gave Himself for me" (Galatians 2:20).

The basis of this request for God's tender mercies is the writer's delight in God's law. It is those that love God, as He has revealed Himself through His Word, that God gives life to in this particular way. Of course, God is the source of life for every man and every creature in a general way, but He particularly gives and sustains life for His children.

Verse 78: "Let the proud be ashamed, for they treated me wrongfully with falsehood; but I will meditate on Your precepts."

God witnesses injustice!

The proud think highly of themselves and want everybody else to think highly of them as well. Proverbs 16:18 reminds us that:

> "Pride goes before destruction, and a haughty spirit before a fall."

In fact, the book of Proverbs has a great deal to say about the proud, and none of it is good! The essence of the proud man is that he thinks himself to be important, relies on himself and his own resources, and therefore feels no need of God.

This takes us right back to the fall of mankind when Adam declared human independence from God and set himself up as a kind of rival to God's sovereignty of His own universe. Shame is the very antithesis of how the proud feels, and yet the writer asks that the proud be ashamed. They should be ashamed because they treated the psalmist badly with no justification. Let's face it, sometimes we deserve the poor treatment we receive. We do not always do what is honest and proper. We can even do the *right* thing in a proud and haughty manner and so alienate other people. Our aim should be to live in the manner described in Titus 2:7-8:

> "In all things showing yourself to be a pattern of good works; in doctrine showing integrity, reverence, incorruptibility, sound speech that cannot be condemned, that one who is an opponent may be ashamed, having nothing evil to say of you."

It is best if others have nothing evil to say about us, but sometimes they will still speak evil of us anyway. 1 Peter 3:16 covers this situation:

> "Having a good conscience, that when they defame you as evildoers, those who revile your good conduct in Christ may be ashamed."

Our enemies should have nothing they can rightfully accuse us of. They will either be ashamed that they can find no accusation, or ashamed that their accusations are unfounded, and that they are criticising what is good and right. In either case, our response should not be to complain, or to gloat, but to meditate on or consider thoughtfully God's Word. It is meditating like this that will both help us live in ways that give no cause for accusation, because our life is being shaped by God's Word, and also ensure that we can face any accusations calmly should they come, knowing we can trust God to maintain our reputation and plead our cause.

Verse 79: "Let those who fear You turn to me, those who know Your testimonies."

Others turn to me!

This verse contains similar thoughts to verse 74. It is about our impact on other believers, but in verse 79 the impact is more active. Verse 74 states the position rather passively:

> "Those who fear You will be glad when they see me."

Verse 79 views the others being more active:

> "Let those who fear You turn to me."

They are visualised as actively turning to the psalmist. This seems to be for fellowship and active support, rather than simply being encouraged by his experiences with God as in verse 74. So how much do people want to fellowship with me?! Do they find it a positive experience? This is not about being "men-pleasers" or compromising to make people like us. Being genuinely like the Lord Jesus will make other Christians want to spend time with us. I read in some Bible study notes recently, the story of a man who had travelled a long way from home and was looking forward to a meal with friends of friends who lived in that area. As they welcomed him in, he immediately felt a sense of peace. He felt at home, comfortable and valued. Later, as he wondered why he had felt so much at home in a strange place, he read 2 Corinthians 2:15, in which Paul says:

> "We are to God the fragrance of Christ among those who are being saved".

"That is it", the man said to himself, "they smelled like Christ!" That man is still telling the story forty years on!

Let us not be doctrinally right, but cold, hard, and unapproachable. Do not compromise at every turn to please everybody. Be faithful to Christ, while being gentle, kind and showing genuine love. That will attract the right people for the right reasons. Those who know God's Word and character will be attracted to us. The flip side is in 2 Corinthians 2:16:

> "To [those who are perishing] we are the aroma of death leading to death, and to [those who are being saved] the aroma of life leading to life".

I dread to think what the aroma of death might be – what a dreadful stench! But that is how we will appear to those who want nothing to do with Christ and are determined to reject Him.

Verse 80: "Let my heart be blameless regarding Your statutes, that I may not be ashamed."

I SHOULD BE BLAMELESS!

As we noted earlier, the psalmist is never satisfied with a knowledge of God's Word that does not get worked out in how he lives. He wants, not just to *know* God's statutes but to be blameless concerning them. In fact, not just the outward details of his life to be blameless but his heart as well. Previously, the writer requested that the proud be

120

ashamed. Now he requests that he *not* be ashamed himself. We should always remember that it is frighteningly easy for us to fall into any number of sins. If we condemn the proud while exhibiting pride ourselves, we are both hypocritical and self-deluding. The psalmist recognised this possibility and prayed that he be kept from shame. The only way to achieve that is to be kept from fault, hence his request for his heart to be blameless. I am sure he was under no illusions about being able to reach some higher spiritual state where it would not be possible for him to sin! In effect he is asking the LORD to keep him from failure in the spirit of Jude 24:

> "To Him who is able to keep you from stumbling, and to present you faultless before the presence of His glory with exceeding joy".

Knowing that he will, no doubt, have to return to the Lord for His "merciful kindness" (verse 76) when he next slips.

Several New Testament verses talk about our ultimate condition of being blameless at the Lord's return. Examples are:

- "Now may the God of peace Himself sanctify you completely; and may your whole spirit, soul and body be preserved blameless at the coming of our Lord Jesus Christ" (1 Thessalonians 5:23).

- "[The] Lord Jesus Christ, who will also confirm you to the end, that you may be blameless in the day of our Lord Jesus Christ" (1 Corinthians 1:8).

We might be tempted to think we should aim a bit lower while we are still living in this world! However, Philippians 2:14-15 cuts across such thoughts:

> "Do all things without complaining and disputing, that you may become blameless and harmless, children of God without fault in the midst of a crooked and perverse generation, among whom you shine as lights in the world".

Clearly, there is a kind of perfect blamelessness that awaits the Lord's return and our new bodies, but there is also a level of being blameless and without fault that we should definitely be aiming at here and now. It is part of our testimony in a world that lives in a totally different way, and should point people towards God, whether they accept Him or not.

Conclusion

We should always thank our God and Father that His Word contains all that we need for our instruction, correction, and encouragement, in order that we might know how to live in a way that pleases Him. Let us have the same thirst for, and delight in, His Word as the psalmist, who lived so long ago. God has not changed in the slightest since then and is as reliable and lovingly tender as He ever was. Indeed, through the Lord and the indwelling Holy Spirit, we can know Him in ways that the psalmist could never have imagined. May our lives reflect such knowledge and such grace!

כ

11. KAPH – verses 81-88

DAVID M HUGHES

Introduction

Many people regard the Bible as irrelevant and say that its moral guidance should not to be taken seriously. It is categorised by them as a useful example of old English literature, of how people used to think long ago. Well, despite the loud claims of many in public life today, the experience of millions of Christians, both today and throughout the ages, is that in fact the Bible is entirely relevant for us. Far from being outdated and a dusty relic, believers have found that it contains absolutely relevant and up-to-date words. They would agree with the Apostle Paul who said that:

> "The word of God is living and powerful,
> and sharper than any two-edged sword"
> (Hebrews 4:12).

In the context of the whole of Psalm 119, verses 81-88 are one of the darkest stanzas of the psalm. It is all about someone who is in desperate need of comfort in the face of intense persecution. Where could he turn? He turned to God's Word. What an important lesson that is for us today. Many people around us might feel that the Bible is fine for learning quaint moral lessons, or for teaching us some nice stories. But they would not dream of reading it and meditating on what it says in times of intense persecution. After all, they would be too busy trying to work their way out of whatever problems they were enduring.

What an opportunity they were missing! What a resource they were turning their back on! According to the Psalmist, they should keep God's Word at the very centre of their thinking, even in intense suffering, and it should be the source of their hope. Countless Christians through the ages would agree and in very difficult times have found encouragement and strength in the Scriptures.

In this stanza of Psalm 119, we learn to keep God's Word central in our lives and to be challenged to think about what the Bible says, even during difficult times. My prayer for all my readers is that we will be helped and blessed; and that we would come to see that the Bible, God's Word to us, is a source of hope and encouragement in life and not some useless dusty relic.

The Psalms do not tend to break down into neat little sections in the way some of the New Testament epistles do. That is not surprising since they were written as poetry. But in verses 81-88, there are four responses to God's Word that will help us to endure difficult circumstances:

1. In verses 81-82, we are told to *hope* in God's Word.

2. In verses 83-85 the challenge is to *remember* God's Word – there are things not to forget whilst we endure suffering.

3. Verses 86-87 teach us to *treasure* God's Word.

4. Verses 88 reminds us to *keep* God's Word.

Verses 81-82: "My soul faints for Your salvation, but I hope in Your word. My eyes fail from searching Your word, saying, 'When will You comfort me?'"

HOPE IN GOD'S WORD

The psalmist was enduring great suffering:

- "My soul faints for Your salvation" (verse 81a).

- "My eyes fail from searching Your word" (verse 82a).

Whatever circumstances he was in the middle of they were certainly difficult. Difficult enough to make the psalmist feel as though he was fainting. He had run out of strength. Difficult enough to make the psalmist say that his eyes were failing for looking out for signs of God's deliverance. He was constantly looking out for some end to his circumstances, some evidence that God would intervene to help him. He longed for some salvation from God. In verses 81-82, we are not being told about some mildly difficult circumstance, the kind that we might face that tire us out for a day or two. Instead the psalmist is describing the exhaustion his whole being was enduring in those difficult days. He longed for relief from the suffering he experienced. Even in such intense suffering, the psalmist reacts:

"I hope in Your word" (verse 81b).

The Psalmist has been clear that, as far as he was concerned, no help had come to him in his suffering. There was no sign of any respite any time soon. That is why he says that his eyes were failing looking for the coming of the help God had promised in His Word. That is why he has to cry out:

> "When will You comfort me?" (verse 82b).

You can hear the longing in that question. And yet, in spite of all this, the psalmist does not lose faith in God. He does not give up on trusting God. No, he says:

> "I hope in Your word" (verse 81b).

What a statement of faith!

- No matter the difficulty: "I hope in Your word."
- No matter how far off help seems: "I hope in Your word."
- No matter how alone and exhausted he may feel: "I hope in Your word."

Does that sound impossible or unrealistic to you? Could the Bible contain sufficient hope for us that if we were experiencing all the circumstances that caused the psalmist's soul to faint, we would say with the psalmist: "I hope in Your word"?

The psalmist was confident that God would keep His promises. He was confident that God would help him; and that God knew best how and when that help should come. That does not come easily. Later, in verse 84, we see that even whilst he was waiting with this hope in God's Word, he frequently calls out to God asking:

- "How many are the days?"

- "When will You execute judgment?"

The fact that the psalmist ultimately had this hope in God's Word and confidence that God knew best, did not stop him wondering and questioning whilst the suffering continued. But the important point for us to see here is that he did not give up on God! He did not stop believing the promises of the Scriptures.

When we face hardship, it can be easy to feel as though God has forgotten about us – that He does not care and that all of His promises somehow do not apply to us. Do not believe that lie of the devil! Do not be tempted to throw your Bible into the bin at the first sign of trouble. In fact, those are the times when, more than ever, we need to read the Bible. We need to be reminded of God's great love for us. We need to be reminded of the greatness of the Lord Jesus, and the wonder of all He has done for us, and all that has been accomplished for us by His death on the cross. We need to be reminded that one day God will judge all sin, one day all wrong will be dealt with righteously and justly and fairly. We need to be reminded that through all of the circumstances of life, God promises to be with His people, to help them and guide them. We need to be reminded of these things and place our hope in them.

So, can I encourage you to hope in God's Word? Read it. Let the truths it contains firmly take root in your mind and your heart. And when difficult times come, do not throw away your Bible, hope in God's Word.

Verses 83-85: "For I have become like a wineskin in smoke, yet I do not forget Your statutes. How many are the days of Your servant? When will You execute judgment on those who persecute me? The proud have dug pits for me, which is not according to Your law."

REMEMBER GOD'S WORD

In verses 83-85, we can see again the intensity of the suffering the psalmist felt. The reference to being like a "wineskin in smoke" is probably a reference to the animal skins that the people in those days used to store wine in. When these were empty and left to hang in a room, the smoke from the house fire, and the heat in the house would dry out the skin and cause it to shrivel up so that they would not be much use for carrying wine anymore. That was how the psalmist felt. The suffering he endured seemed to have so affected him that he felt all dried up, all the life sucked out of him, so that he felt shrivelled up like this wineskin bottle. Calvin says that he was, "parched by the continual heat of adversities"[15].

The psalmist carries on by asking:

"How many are the days?" (verse 84b).

- "How long will I suffer like this?"
- "How long will it be before You stop those who persecute me?"

Ungodly people were causing the psalmist trouble. These people had no interest in God's law. They were out to trap

[15] John Calvin, *Commentary on the Book of Psalms*, Volume IV, page 375, translated by John Anderson, Edinburgh: The Edinburgh Printing Company, 1847

him. Would God not intervene and help him? We can sense some of the psalmist's anguish in verses 83-85.

Waiting for anything is hard. Have you noticed how easy it is to get frustrated waiting in a traffic jam? Or how hard it is for young children to wait until Christmas day once they see presents accumulating by the Christmas tree? Smartphones and the internet are great tools, but perhaps you easily become impatient waiting for someone to respond to an e-mail or text? If waiting for fairly trivial things is hard, it is so much harder to wait for the end of difficult times. It is not easy to wait patiently for a loved one's suffering to end. It is not easy to wait until the end of some difficult period at work, or in family life. We can begin to understand the difficulties the psalmist faced as he waited for his suffering to end. It was hard! But in all of his waiting, the psalmist did not forget God's statutes. He *remembered* God's Word. We have already considered how he hoped in God's Word. Now we are reminded that he did not forget it!

When struggling, do not forget what God says in His Word. Instead remember it and allow God's Word to give perspective to all that you are enduring. Meditate on God's promises and let them encourage you and point you away from your circumstances and towards the almighty and all loving God, who stands beside you in your suffering. I read a quote once that said something like:

> "Do not forget in the darkness what God
> has taught you in the light."

There is something in that! The things you know about God today, will not be any less true tomorrow when you endure hardship of whatever kind. God is not any less able to help you in difficulty than He is in good times. When the dark times come, when your soul faints and longs for God's salvation, remember God's promises.

Elisabeth Elliot, the missionary and author, whose husband was killed as he tried to take the good news of the Gospel to jungle tribes in Ecuador said:

> "If He died to let us live in His company,
> is He likely to abandon us just because
> things look dark?"[16]

So then, always remember that God has already acted to bring you the best salvation. He has already sent His Son to bear the judgment for your sins. The Lord Jesus has already intervened, not to save you from the consequences of some ungodly people, but from the consequences of your own sin. He has not just delivered you from some sticky patch, but from eternal judgment for sin. No wonder the writer to the Hebrews writes of this as "so great salvation" (Hebrews 2:3). Consider if God has cared for you and me so much that He has provided this wonderful and great salvation, with not just temporary, but eternal consequences, do you not think that He will be with you in the trials and suffering we face in life? Do not forget in the dark what you have learnt in the light!

Of course, this all assumes that you have learnt something in the first place. You cannot forget what you do not know. Hence the importance of reading the Bible. If we do not take the time to read, think about and learn the Scriptures, what will the Holy Spirit be able to remind us of in times of difficulty? We all have busy lives. There

[16] Elisabeth Elliot, *A Lamp for My Feet: The Bible's Light for Daily Living,* Ann Arbor, Michigan: Servant Publications, 1985, page 48.

are always so many things to do. But we must all find some time in our day to read the Scriptures, even if that is only a small part of each day. It is amazing how much you can take in over time just by reading a few verses a day, thinking about them, trying to apply them to your own life, and enjoying the truths they contain in your own heart. Perhaps, like me, you are not currently enduring much difficulty compared to the experiences described by the psalmist in this stanza. But perhaps the Lord will use some of the verses we read this week to prepare us for difficulties we may face in the future. Or perhaps when we do face suffering, the Lord will remind us of something we have previously read, and He will use it to help us. We must read the Scriptures!

Verses 86-87: "All Your commandments are faithful; they persecute me wrongfully; help me! They almost made an end of me on earth, but I did not forsake Your precepts."

TREASURE GOD'S WORD

- Verses 81-82 reminded us to *hope* in God's Word.
- Verses 83-85 reminded us to *remember* God's Word.
- Verses 86-87 teach us to *treasure* God's Word.

On first glance, verse 86 seems a bit strange. Why are God's commandments described as faithful? Perhaps just or right or perfect might have been more understandable. I think the Psalmist saw all of God's laws as a testimony to His faithfulness. They reminded him, by the fact that God's laws had a "rightness" about them, that God was and is always faithfully interested in the best for His people. He always wants good things for them, and He sovereignly knows what those good things would be. The psalmist knew that God would be faithful to keep His commandments. Faithful obedience would be rewarded whereas sinful disobedience would be judged and punished. God was and is faithful, and it must be so. So even though the psalmist was enduring very hard circumstances, he could look at God's commands and be reminded that those who persecuted him would be held to account by God for their sins, and that God would help him at just the right time. So the psalmist treasures God's commands. He views them almost like faithful promises and is able to await God's deliverance at the right time. For the time being, he is content to simply say, "Help me".

Do we similarly treasure God's commandments? Do we love them enough to appreciate that they are right and are a reminder of God's faithfulness? As we, like the psalmist, endure difficult times, do we remember the commandments of God and by faith believe that God will send the necessary help at just the right time?

Then in verse 87, we are reminded that even though the psalmist's circumstances were so severe that they had almost made an end of him, he had not forsaken God's precepts. He had not given up on God and His Word, even though times were more difficult than most believers will ever have to endure.

When life is difficult, we might be tempted to give up on the instructions of the Bible. After all, sometimes it seems as though, if we were just willing to compromise our obedience to God and His Word, then our difficulties would be over so quickly. Would not it just be easier to ignore some small part of the Scriptures? That would be the advice of so many today. Just discard some small, seemingly inconsequential part of the Bible and some of your problems will disappear. The psalmist did not think like that. Even though his difficulties almost made an end of him, he did not forsake God's precepts. Will you? Do you treasure God's Word so much that you will cling to it and not forsake it, no matter what? Will you look for comfort and help in the Scriptures no matter how hard the challenges you face?

Notice the little encouragement in verse 87:

> "They almost made an end of me on earth."

"Almost"! But not quite! In spite of the fact that the psalmist endured such terrible circumstances, the worst that they could do to him was to "almost" make an end of him. That was the extent of the psalmist's confidence in God and in His Word. The very worst that the world could do to him was to almost destroy him. But he had confidence that God would deliver him in whatever way God knew was best.

That is a good point to keep in mind as we endure hardship in life. The very worst that circumstances can do is to "almost" destroy us. The very worst that people around us can do is to "almost" make an end of us. If we are believers and have faith in Christ, then our hope in God is so great that it can endure even the worst the world can throw at us.

Many Christians have died as a result of their faith. Elisabeth Elliot's husband, Jim, was killed taking the Gospel to people who had never heard it before. He once said:

> "He is no fool who gives up what he
> cannot keep to gain what he cannot
> lose."[17]

That is how much Jim treasured the salvation he received from God. That is how much it affected his life. I suspect that he would have agreed with the psalmist that the worst that can happen is that he be almost destroyed. Jim's faith really did cost him his life, but the risk of that happening did not stop him trusting God and trying to reach people with the good news of salvation in Jesus Christ. He valued his eternal inheritance more even than his own life. He did not forsake God's Word.

Remember, when you endure hard times as a believer, you have a great hope that endures even beyond this life. Your hope is of spending all eternity with Jesus Christ our Lord. How wonderful that will be! The worst that hardship can bring to us is temporary to this life. That is not in any way to minimise the terrible suffering that many believers in the world endure. I cannot begin to imagine how some believers endure the hardships they face. The only answer must be that they, like the psalmist, have learnt to love God's Word and find comfort in it.

Warren Wiersbie wrote:

> "When the Father allows His children to
> go through the furnace of affliction, He
> keeps His eye on the clock and His hand
> on the thermostat. He knows how long
> and how much."[18]

[17] Elisabeth Elliot, *Through Gates of Splendor*, New York: Harper & Brothers, 1957, page 172.
[18] Warren W. Wiersbie, *The Bible exposition commentary: The Old Testament: Wisdom and Poetry*, Cook Communications Ministries, Colorado Springs, Colorado, USA, 2004, page 322.

Circumstances may seem to be overwhelming, like they were in the psalmist's day. But God cares for His people. He will not abandon them. Keep that in mind always.

Verse 88: "Revive me according to Your lovingkindness, so that I may keep the testimony of Your mouth."

KEEPING GOD'S WORD

We have already seen that the psalmist found help in God's Word in difficult times. Now this stanza ends with a prayer for help. He needed help from God to be able to keep God's commandments. He needed to be revived. How good that he was not asking for help from some mean-spirited source. Interestingly, he asked for help instead "according to Your lovingkindness." In spite of the fact that the psalmist had endured such hardship that his soul fainted, he still thought of God as being lovingly kind to him. Even during great persecution, the psalmist still saw evidences of ways that God had been kind to him and loving towards him. And it is to this lovingly kind God that he now appeals for help. How crucial that is for us if we are to endure hardship and faithfully keep God's Word. Look for evidences day by day of how God has been kind to you. Treasure reminders that God loves you. Keep them often in your thinking. And as you do so, look to God for fresh help daily to keep His Word.

Responding faithfully to all that life throws at us is not easy. Living in a way that honours God can be hard, especially if people set out to make that difficult for us. But we are not left alone to do so. We have a God who is characterised by lovingkindness, ready to help us. We have a God who has already shown us the greatest lovingkindness in giving His only begotten Son for us. Do we think that He will not then help us to keep His Word and live faithfully in difficult days? Let us always remember how Paul put it in Romans 8:32:

> "He who did not spare His own Son, but delivered Him up for us all, how shall He not with Him also freely give us all things?"

So ask for help. Look to our lovingly kind God today and ask for help to keep His Word and live faithfully, in a way that honours Him, no matter what circumstances you face. Take comfort from the experience of the psalmist in Psalm 119:81-88. It is an experience that was, is and will be shared by countless believers throughout the ages. No matter what circumstances you face, always look to God's Word. May our lovingly kind God help us:

1. *Hope* in it.
2. *Remember* it.
3. *Treasure* it.
4. *Keep* it.

ל

12. LAMED – verses 89-96

David G Pulman

Introduction

In the original Hebrew Scriptures, each verse of this stanza commences with the Hebrew letter LAMED, which means "ox-goad". In the hand of a farmer ploughing, or a cart driver, the ox-goad would be used to start and keep the oxen going forward, ensure they keep moving in the right direction and maybe even encouraged to quicken their pace. Over the years, I have often been reminded that in Christian development there is never the thought of standing still or going backwards as this would result in spiritual stagnation. Christianity is always connected with progress, growing and spiritual development. As Paul states:

> "I press toward the goal for the prize of
> the upward call of God in Christ Jesus"
> (Philippians 3:14).

Verse 89: "Forever, O Lᴏʀᴅ, Your word is settled in heaven."

This short verse contains some important issues. First, the word "forever" indicates to us that the Lord's Word is eternal and established in heaven. His Word is communicated to us by God's servants as inspired by the Holy Spirit:

> "All Scripture is given by inspiration of God, and is profitable for doctrine, for reproof, for correction, for instruction in righteousness, that the man of God may be complete, thoroughly equipped for every good work" (2 Timothy 3:16-17).

God's Word is permanent and is not subject to change. So, His Word is dependable; we can always rely upon its teaching. God's Word equips us for godly service and provides us with daily guidance. Finally, we should emphasise that it is the Lord's Word which is preserved for us in the Bible. His Word is not a 'pick and mix' of our own choosing. If His Word does not fit with the standards of the world, then the only conclusion for a Christian is that His Word is right, and that the world has got it wrong!

Verse 90: "Your faithfulness endures to all generations; You established the earth, and it abides."

The first part of verse 90 directs our attention back to God:

> "Your faithfulness endures to all generations."

In many ways God is faithful, especially faithful to those who believe. From Adam onwards, from one generation to the next, God's faithfulness can be traced as we read through the Bible. Where there is failure, it is on our side, but God remains faithful and constant throughout. God does not change and neither does His "Word". The second part of verse 90 brings to our attention God's wonderful creation:

"You established the earth, and it abides."

We are taken right back to the beginning of time – Genesis 1-2.

When we read the book of Genesis, we know that problems and difficulties occurred. Disobedience and sin arrived with a devastating impact and had dramatic consequences (see Genesis 3:1-24). The perfection of creation became damaged, and the once ideal environment changed to a disastrous situation. The flood (see Genesis 6:1-9:17) was the next major disaster for mankind when God judged the evil of people with only eight persons being preserved (see 1 Peter 3:20). But through it all, the basic work of creation remained, the established earth abides – it endures, it continues. This is the major point of God's faithfulness to all generations of mankind.

Verse 91: "They continue this day according to Your ordinances, for all are Your servants."

The psalmist states that God's Word and creation continue right up to this day. It is not just to the psalmist's day but to our day; and they will continue because God's Word is settled in heaven and the decision about creation is in the hand of God:

"While the earth remains, seedtime and harvest, cold and heat, winter and summer, and day and night shall not cease" (Genesis 8:22).

Still today these basic conditions of creation remain in the calendar of each year.

God's Word reveals all that we need to know about divine Persons, God the Father, God the Son and God the Holy Spirit. This is what we have in the Bible, God's revealed Word. God's Word is unlike the words of mankind which cannot reach into the soul and bring people to a saving faith in Christ, the Son of God.

Creation is the platform in which God has displayed His wonderful love and grace to the whole of mankind. From the amazing expanse of the universe as seen on a clear starry night to the microscopic detail within a single cell. Most amazing of all is the tremendous event of the incarnation of the Son of God.

All has been divinely decided according to God's ordinances or judgments. What has been established cannot change. The latest concern that the environmentalists have is the damage being caused to the planet by plastic waste. The wonder product of decades ago is now a monster damaging the environment. Some plastic is not bio-degradable, it simply breaks up into smaller and smaller pieces. In recent times we have seen rivers choked with plastic rubbish, beaches totally covered with plastic and vast floating islands of plastic in the world's oceans. Mankind seems to have an aptitude to be destructive!

Verse 92: "Unless Your law had been my delight, I would then have perished in my affliction."

When the psalmist uses the word "law" he is considering the whole of God's Word. God's Word is there to teach, to give daily guidance and to direct our attention towards right things. God's Word is an anchor, or foundation stone, on which to build our lives. This verse shows the psalmist delighting in the law; he finds joy in reading and, no doubt, meditating on God's Word. We must challenge ourselves as to whether we find delight in reading the Bible.

We are not told specifically about the affliction that the psalmist was going through. The word in the Hebrew is associated with poverty, misery and even depression. It would seem to be life threatening as he talks about perishing, even to losing his life. Let us not miss the 'lifesaving' connection. The Word of God is much undervalued in the world today. God's Word provides the balance and solutions to life's problems.

Verse 93: "I will never forget Your precepts, for by them You have given me life."

Verse 93 supports and emphasises what has been said in connection with verse 92. The psalmist makes a binding promise to his God:

> "I will never forget Your precepts."

It is good to make a commitment to God's Word. Read God's Word daily and memorise what you can. Daily reading God's Word is important for every Christian. It is the daily spiritual manna that has its origin in heaven.

141

A precept is that which is a specific charge for which we are expected to be responsible. God gave the Israelites ten commandments (see Exodus 20:1-17). Each commandment was a specific charge for them to obey. The Israelites had asked God to give them commandments, but they discovered it was impossible to keep them. However, that was not a valid reason not to commit to live by them to the best of their ability. It was this kind of life God desired from His earthly people.

What was missing in every Israelite was the power to live fully by God's Word. It is so different in the Christian age. The indwelling Holy Spirit in every believer gives the ability to live a godly life – to refuse the wrong and to do the right. Paul found he had two conflicting natures. Romans 7:24-25 highlight the problem. Romans 7:24 states:

> "O wretched man that I am! Who will deliver me from this body of death?"

Paul concluded that the natural man has not the power to do what is right for God. But the remedy in Romans 7:25 states:

> "I thank God – through Jesus Christ our Lord! So then, with the mind I myself serve the law of God, but with the flesh the law of sin."

The realisation that two principles are at work is a major step forward, which every Christian needs to understand. We are not left at this point for Romans 8:1-4 complete the teaching on how to live a victorious life:

142

- Romans 8:1 gives the principle that is true for every person who has trusted the Lord Jesus Christ as their Saviour and Lord:

> "There is therefore now no condemnation to those who are in Christ Jesus".

Our sins are forgiven, and the judgment due to us has been taken by Jesus on the cross. We are now in a place of blessing.

- Romans 8:2-4 teach how a believer can now live a victorious Spirit filled and controlled life:

> "For the law of the Spirit of life in Christ Jesus has made me free from the law of sin and death. For what the law could not do in that it was weak through the flesh, God did by sending His own Son in the likeness of sinful flesh, on account of sin: He condemned sin in the flesh, that the righteous requirement of the law might be fulfilled in us who do not walk according to the flesh but according to the Spirit."

This power (of the permanent indwelling of the Holy Spirit in Christians today) was not true of the godly Israelite of old. The Holy Spirit came upon godly Israelites, but it was not permanent as it is with Christians. As King David of old said in Psalm 51:11:

> "Do not cast me away from Your presence, and do not take Your Holy Spirit from me."

This cannot happen to a true believer in the Lord Jesus Christ.

Verse 94: "I am Yours, save me; for I have sought Your precepts."

This verse continues the same thoughts as verses 92-93. The psalmist is obviously concerned about the situation that was threatening to engulf him. In verse 92, he was in danger of perishing or dying, whereas in verse 93 he was looking for life. Once again in verse 94 there is the cry, "save me." In many respects this person is desperate. But instead of looking around for someone or something to help, he remains firm as to God's Word. Again, he states that he is seeking God's precepts. There is a plea to God; he reminds God of his personal faithfulness to God's Word. Because he is living a godly life, then this is the basis for God to intervene and bring about deliverance.

We might think that God is either deaf to the psalmist's entreaties or uncaring as to the situation of one of His own children. Both thoughts are untrue. 1 Corinthians 10:13 is a wonderful verse:

> "No temptation has overtaken you except such as is common to man; but God is faithful, who will not allow you to be tempted beyond what you are able, but with the temptation will also make the way of escape, that you may be able to bear it."

We are likely to face many temptations or trials as we go through life. Just because we belong eternally to God does not guarantee a life free from difficulty. Some difficulties may be of our own making and others may come upon us from external situations. The challenge is, "How do we respond to the trials?" 1 Corinthians 10:13 showed the boundaries and limits. When they were younger, my son used to take his two children camping and not always in the best of weather! He felt that this was one of the ways to develop their character – "character forming", he would say. (He was probably following his parents who also went camping with their three children!)

In verses 92-94, we have noticed how the psalmist refers to the law and specifically to precepts in the law. This was the bedrock on which the psalmist stood. He was not going to move away from this secure place; it was his stronghold. There is a similar theme in Psalm 61:2:

> "From the end of the earth I will cry to
> You, when my heart is overwhelmed; lead
> me to the rock that is higher than I."

The teaching in God's Word is not theoretical but it is very practical, both in meeting the circumstances of daily life and in developing godly character.

Verse 95: "The wicked wait for me to destroy me, but I will consider Your testimonies."

In verse 95, we now move from the generalisation of the "afflictions" that the psalmist spoke of in verse 92 to the identification of persons, "the wicked". It is these persons who are greatly disturbing the psalmist. We are not told what it is about, but in every age the wicked, or ungodly, do not need a reason to persecute believers. Just after sin came into the world through Adam's failure and disobedience (see Genesis 2:17-3:7), we find Cain murdering his brother Abel and lying to God about the whole affair. Abel had not wronged Cain, but Cain was angry with God and took out his anger on his own brother, Abel (see Genesis 4:1-15).

Notice the language of verse 95a:

"The wicked wait for me to destroy me."

They were looking for an occasion, probably when there were no witnesses, so that they could carry out their evil intentions. In the above situation of Cain and Abel, Cain probably thought no one had seen his evil crime but God had observed the whole event. Non-Christians think that wrongs can be hidden but God always sees and even knows the motives. Also, God has His day of reckoning when all things will be judged according to His divine standard. The psalmist knew that God understands and sees all, that everything is written down in God's records. The Scriptures are full of information about the nature of God:

- John states that "God is love" (1 John 4:8 and 16).
- Psalm 99:9 states: "For the LORD our God is holy."
- Daniel 9:14 states: "For the LORD our God is righteous."

We might think these attributes are conflicting but not with God:

- God's nature of love is seen in the Lord Jesus Christ, His atoning death and resurrection to the throne of grace in heaven.
- God's holiness means that He cannot be associated with sin nor allow it and sinners to escape His justice – even to the point of eternal punishment in the lake of fire.

- God's righteousness enables Him to bring into blessing those who trust Christ as Saviour to have their sins forgiven and to condemn those who refuse or ignore God's offer of mercy.

The psalmist knows his God, understands the testimonies found in the Scriptures and therefore places his confidence in what he knows:

"But I will consider Your testimonies" (verse 95b).

How do we gain such confidence or assurance? The answer is:

"By taking heed according to Your word" (verse 9).

Verse 96: "I have seen the consummation of all perfection, but Your commandment is exceedingly broad."

At first sight, verse 96 seems a little difficult but I think it is a contrast. The psalmist observes the world in which he lives and sees that any perfection that might seemingly have been achieved has its end or limit:

- In Young's Literal Translation of the Scriptures, he rephrases the first part of verse 96 as: "Of all perfection I have seen an end" (YLT), which makes the whole verse easier to understand.

- "Your commandment is exceedingly broad" (verse 96b) indicates that the Scriptures have a quality to them which cannot be exhausted regardless of how much study is undertaken.

It is God's intention that Christians grow in spiritual maturity. In Philippians 3:10, Paul states:

"That I may know Him, and the power of His resurrection, and the fellowship of His sufferings, being conformed to His death".

Reading further in Philippians 3, we find Paul was always striving forward to gain a better appreciation of Christ (see verses 12-15). In Philippians 1:21, he states:

"For to me, to live is Christ, and to die is gain."

Striving or moving forward in faith seems to be Paul's motivation in his Christian service. What he desired for himself he undoubtedly desired for fellow believers.

Conclusions

1. Verses 89-96 have focused our attention on the Hebrew letter LAMED, meaning ox-goad.

2. We have seen that God's Word is firmly established and continues unchanging (verses 89-91).

3. In verses 92-95, we have the repeated preserving and life-giving qualities of God's Word brought before us.

4. Finally, in verse 96, we have indicated the inexhaustible quality of the Scriptures. This reminds me of the river that flows out from the House of God in Ezekiel 47. As Ezekiel walked into the river, he found waters to swim in, and it was so broad that it could not be crossed (see Ezekiel 47:5).

5. As the ox-goad encourages and guides the oxen forward may God's Word motivate us to move forward to grow spiritually.

מ

13.   MEM – verses 97-104

IAN D BRITTON

Introduction

Over 40 years ago I read a library book which claimed
that many common over the counter medicines and
beauty treatments are totally ineffective. The one that
seems to have stuck in my mind referred to anti-dandruff
shampoos – do not ask me why! Before the makers of
such products issue any lawsuits, I point out that I am
simply passing on the writer's statements: I have no
evidence to offer either way! The author claimed that
while the chemicals in most anti-dandruff shampoos may
have some benefit, they will never work if you simply
apply the shampoo and then wash it back off again, as
they recommend on the label. They can only work, he
claimed, if you leave then on your hair much longer than
anybody normally does.

Our way of handling God's Word can often suffer from
the same problem this long-forgotten author was
describing. We read it, apply it very briefly to our minds,
and then it is "rinsed away" by our busy lives before it has

any chance to achieve its intended purpose! Not so with the writer of Psalm 119!

Verse 97: "Oh, how I love Your law! It is my meditation all the day."

This is the fifth out of seven times that the writer uses the words "meditate" or "meditation" in this psalm.[19] It was plainly important to him. In the first verse of this stanza he links the meditation with his love of God's Word. The reason that he meditates on God's Word is because he loves it. He runs it over and over again in his mind, like the words of a letter from a well-loved friend. For some of us the word meditation conjures up images of eastern mystics emptying their minds by focussing on something repetitive and mundane, but the Bible meaning is about *filling* our minds with something valuable and beautiful. By definition, it takes time, which is one of the scarcest resources in many of our lives. But it is not just a question of finding a few more minutes to add to our daily Bible reading time. The psalmist talks about "all the day." I do not think he meant he just sat around for a whole day quietly contemplating a passage of Scripture. I assume that as he went through his day, whenever his tasks allowed him a few minutes to think things over, he went back to considering God's Word. I am sure it had become a habit for him. The whole of this long psalm gives us evidence of the impact it had on his life, and God's Word is *meant* to have a significant impact on us.

Ezra gives us a perfect example of how we ought to approach the Bible:

> "For Ezra had prepared his heart to seek
> the Law of the LORD, and to do it, and to

---

[19] Others are in verses 15, 23, 48, 78, 99, 148.

teach statutes and ordinances in Israel"
(Ezra 7:10).

There are four stages outlined in this verse and they come
in a certain order.

1. Ezra prepared his heart.
2. Ezra prepared to seek the law.
3. Ezra sought the law to do it.
4. Ezra taught.

1. EZRA PREPARED HIS HEART

There was some desire to understand God's law, but a
realisation that it would not just happen automatically.
Ezra wanted to be ready to meet with God, not through
some complex ritual, but by setting aside some time and
settling his mind ready for the task.

2. EZRA PREPARED TO SEEK THE LAW

Seek, suggests some effort and application. He wanted to
increase his familiarity with what the Word of God said.
After all, the only way to get to know God is to see what
He has revealed about Himself, and by far the best way to
do that is to read His Word. You might describe this as
the building up of knowledge, and a store of information
about God, His character, and His instructions.

3. EZRA SOUGHT THE LAW TO DO IT

This is very much true of the person who wrote Psalm
119. Two things are abundantly clear throughout this
Psalm:

- That the writer does not just *know* God's law, he *does*
  it.
- The writer values God's law, not for its own sake,
  but because it brings him close to the God he loves.

James is very straightforward about the vast chasm between those who just read God's Word, and those who also do it!

> "If anyone is a hearer of the word and not a doer, he is like a man observing his natural face in a mirror; for he observes himself, goes away, and immediately forgets what kind of man he was. But he who looks into the perfect law of liberty and continues in it, and is not a forgetful hearer but a doer of the work, this one will be blessed in what he does" (James 1:23-25).

We are back to the illustration of the anti-dandruff shampoo again! Just hearing has the most transient of impacts on us and we forget immediately. Continuing, which is related to meditating, and doing, are the transformational activities; they make the real difference in our lives and produce the blessing. This takes us beyond knowledge, into wisdom. Wise people do not just know what the Bible says – although they must have that as a minimum – they also know how it applies to their everyday life.

4. EZRA TAUGHT

When he had learned how to apply the Word of God to his own life, he was ready to teach it to other people. As already stated, these four things have a proper order. We obviously cannot *teach* before we *know*, but neither should we presume to teach before we *do* either. Not that a teacher must be faultless but seeking to instruct others in something you are not prepared to do yourself is a very dangerous position to take. Ezra is described, in the book that carries his name, as a "scribe". That means that he was well enough instructed in the Bible to be able to teach and explain it to other people.

At the time that Ezra was written, the title of scribe was a very honourable one. By the time we reach the Gospels, the title has become much less positive. The Gospel writers often group together, "scribes and Pharisees", and have some very harsh things to say about them. The Lord Jesus also:

> "The scribes and the Pharisees sit in Moses seat. Therefore whatever they tell you to observe, that observe and do, but do not do according to their works; for they say, and do not do. For they bind heavy burdens, hard to bear, and lay them on men's shoulders; but they themselves will not move them with one of their fingers. But all their works they do to be seen by men. They make their phylacteries broad and enlarge the borders of their garments. They love the best places at feasts, the best seats in the synagogues, greetings in the marketplaces, and to be called by men, 'Rabbi, Rabbi'" (Matthew 23:2-7).

The word "Rabbi" means teacher. The scribes in Jesus' day wanted to be teachers of the law, but they had very little desire to apply it properly to their own lives! I sometimes like to tease my friends who are members of the teaching profession by quoting the expression, "Those that can do. Those that cannot teach." It may be a little unfair to teachers, but it describes the scribes to a

T! They could not, or rather would not, do what the Law said, but they loved to instruct *others* in it.

Ezra and the writer of Psalm 119 had very different characteristics. Which begs the question, how can you increase learning and knowledge in ways that do not make you a scribe or a Pharisee? The simple answer is, be careful about *why* you want more knowledge and *what* you do with it. Knowledge, even knowledge of God's perfect Word, that is acquired simply to make you look clever and win arguments will, slowly but surely, produce the kind of pride and arrogance that the scribes displayed. Never bothering to pause periodically to check if what you do and say, matches up with what you have learnt, will carry you another step along that pathway. Being much faster to point the finger at other people's failures to carry out what the Bible says than to confess your own lack of obedience, will demonstrate that you are well on track to become one of those people Jesus condemned so vigorously!

In the same way that the medical professionals tell us that we should regularly check our bodies for early warning signs of certain illnesses, we all need to give ourselves a careful spiritual self-examination once in a while! What will we find? Evidence of the kind of good spiritual health which Ezra and the writer of Psalm 119 exhibited? Or some of the tell-tale early warning signs of early onset Phariseeism!

Verses 98-100: "You, through Your commandments, make me wiser than my enemies; for they are ever with me. I have more understanding than all my teachers, for Your testimonies are my meditation. I understand more than the ancients, because I keep Your precepts."

The psalmist makes three striking statements about himself in verses 98-100:

1. "You…make me wiser than my enemies" (verse 98).

2. "I have more understanding than all my teachers" (verse 99).

3. "I understand more than the ancients" (verse 100).

1. "YOU…MAKE ME WISER THAN MY ENEMIES" (VERSE 98)

First, notice where this wisdom comes from. It is God that makes the writer wiser than his enemies, not his own abilities or achievements. The New Testament clearly sets out two kinds of wisdom. 1 Corinthians 1 calls them the "wisdom of this world" (1 Corinthians 1:20) and the "wisdom of God" (1 Corinthians 1:21). James 3 describes a wisdom that is "earthly, sensual [and] demonic" (James 3:15) and contrasts it with a "wisdom that is from above" (James 3:17).

No doubt the psalmist's enemies had some of the first kind of wisdom and would use it to against him constantly. But if he was made wiser by God, this could only be the wisdom of God, which James describes as "first pure, then peaceable, gentle, willing to yield, full of mercy and good fruits, without partiality and without hypocrisy" (James 3:17).

155

At first glance, these seem like pretty feeble weapons to meet enemies with! But they compose the wisdom of God, represent the character of God, and carry the power of God; and *that* power is frequently exhibited in ways that are rather surprising to human beings!

2. "I HAVE MORE UNDERSTANDING THAN ALL MY TEACHERS" (VERSE 99a)

How can you know more than the person who teaches you? It seems counter-intuitive! We ought to be able to have, at the very best, equal understanding to those who instruct us. But when you stop to think about it, if this is not possible, how can progress or revival ever happen? If we were limited to never exceeding our teachers, then knowledge could only ever get less over time. That certainly is not true in the realms of science and technology, and I do not believe that it should be the case in spiritual things either. Things do often decline, but God can send renewal and revival, and we should always want the next generation of believers to surpass us in their knowledge of God and their obedience to His Word. I believe there is such a thing as healthy spiritual ambition, both for others and for ourselves. We should never be content to drift along with no desire for growth or progress. Having more understanding than his teachers is linked to the psalmist's meditation for it is said to be because:

> "Your testimonies are my meditation"
> (verse 99b).

The writer did not just learn some facts from his teachers, he meditated on the things he had learnt about God, and this caused him to grow.

156

3. "I UNDERSTAND MORE THAN THE ANCIENTS" (VERSE 100a)

This is perhaps the most startling claim of the three. Our culture values youth over age, and we are inclined to think of things, and people, declining in value as they get older. The culture in Biblical times was quite different. The old, and things of the past, were highly prized. People looked back to David as the greatest of the kings; and Moses as the greatest of the prophets, and the ancients were the great store of wisdom. To understand more than the ancients is a claim of a very high order! However, it was understood that age does not automatically produce wisdom. Job 32:9 states:

> "Great men are not always wise, nor do
> the aged always understand justice."

Put simply, age creates the opportunity to become wise, but it does not provide a guarantee that it will happen. The more years you have lived, the more opportunities you have had to learn and grow wiser, but not everybody takes those opportunities. We do not know how old the writer of Psalm 119 was, but he had evidently used his time well! The second clause gives us the reason for this high level of understanding: "because I keep your precepts" (verse 100b). And, once again, the point is reinforced that progress in understanding God's Word is built on obeying what we already know.

Verse 101: "I have restrained my feet from every evil way, that I may keep Your word."

The Word of God seeps into our minds through reading and meditation. Then it shapes our thoughts and attitudes, which, in turn, form our behaviours and produce self-control. It is this self-control that is the focus of verse 101. Let us face it, we are all tempted to do what is wrong, and we will quickly succumb to those temptations unless we exercise a healthy self-restraint. Our sinful nature produces wrongdoing without us needing to be very active in the matter. We sin almost automatically. So, if we are to keep God's Word, we will need to keep that sinful nature in check.

The wisdom that God gives to those who meditate on His Word, enables us to restrain our minds from dwelling on wrong thoughts. This will allow us to stop our lips saying wrong things, which, in turn, will prevent our feet from walking in wrong paths.

Verse 102: "I have not departed from Your judgments, for You Yourself have taught me."

Verse 102 reminds us who our ultimate Teacher is; and where our real strength comes from. The reason the psalmist has been able to keep God's commandments is because of the understanding and wisdom that God Himself has taught him. We have noticed in other stanzas of this psalm, that the writer is not claiming sinless perfection for himself. It is clear that there have been times when he has gone astray and had to seek God's forgiveness and restoration. What he means here is that any faithfulness he has shown in keeping God's Word, has been the result of God's instruction and power.

Verse 103: "How sweet are Your words to my taste, sweeter than honey to my mouth!"

This stanza opened with the words:

"Oh, how I love Your law!" (verse 97a).

Now the psalmist evidently delights in God's Word and derives genuine pleasure from it. You do not get the impression of a man who slogged his way dutifully through a daily Bible reading, all the time longing for something a bit less dreary! The reference to honey reminds me of the time when King Saul's son, Jonathan, was involved in a long battle, and feeling weary:

> "But Jonathan ... stretched out the end of the rod that was in his hand and dipped it in a honeycomb, and put his hand to his mouth; and his countenance brightened" (1 Samuel 14:27).

The honey seemed to incorporate: sweetness, refreshing, and strength.

SWEETNESS

Honey is known for its sweetness. There are some foods that your mother had to instruct you to eat, "because it is good for you!" Honey is not one of those! You do not hold your nose to get it down, like a foul-tasting medicine. You eat honey to enjoy its delicious sweetness. The psalmist states that God's Word tastes even sweeter to him than honey (verse 103). Of course, a diet of honey alone would not be very healthy! Sometimes, God's Word comes to us with a bitter taste when it challenges our idleness or exposes our sins. The point is, that it can bring joy and delight when we value it properly.

REFRESHING

The honey brightened Jonathan's countenance, that is it refreshed him. Wearied from the battle and its exertions, a little honey lifted his spirits wonderfully. So can the

Word of God refresh us when life is proving a battle, or a weariness.

STRENGTH

Jonathan goes on to make the point that if all the rest of the army had taken suitable nourishment, the victory might have been much greater. Food provides strength for the task at hand. We cannot expect to be very productive in the work God has given us to do, if we are not regularly feeding on His Word He has provided to strengthen us.

Verse 104: "Through Your precepts I get understanding; therefore I hate every false way."

In the last verse of this stanza, we are still engaged with one of its main themes, that of understanding. Now we find that the understanding which comes from God's Word, enables us to distinguish right ways from false ways, and to shun the false ones:

> "There is a way that seems right to a man,
> but its end is the way of death" (Proverbs
> 14:12 & 16:25).

Human wisdom, discussed under verse 98, may conclude that a certain way is right and profitable, but the wisdom of God discerns that it will end in death. Hating such a false way is very sensible and appropriate.

Conclusion

The Hebrew letter that every verse in this stanza starts with is called MEM, which it carries the meaning of water. Water is a well-known picture of God's Word:

> "Christ also loved the church and gave
> Himself for her, that He might sanctify

and cleanse her with *the washing of water by the word*" (Ephesians 5:25-26).

Am I being regularly cleaned up by the careful application of God's Word? Jesus said:

- "Whoever drinks of this water will thirst again, but whoever drinks of the water that I shall give him will never thirst" (John 4:13-14).
- "If anyone thirsts, let him come to Me and drink" (John 7:37).

Are we drinking regularly from the clean water supply that is the Bible?

נ

14.   NUN – verses 105-112

Jonathan Hughes

Introduction

> "The people who walked in darkness have
> seen a great light; those who dwelt in the
> land of the shadow of death, upon them
> a light has shined" (Isaiah 9:2).

Here we have the wonderful promise of the coming
Messiah. Part of His mission was to reveal God to us –
He would be the very embodiment of all that God is. But
He was to come to a people who were walking in
darkness. That is striking in that the nation of Israel were
the most religious nation on earth and without doubt
their moral code was of a far higher order than the
nations around about them.

Sadly, when we come to the fulfilment of this verse in
John's Gospel we read:

- "And the light shines in the darkness, and the
  darkness did not comprehend it" (John 1:5).

- "He came unto His own, and His own did not receive Him" (John 1:11).

As the light of God shone in this world, it was utterly rejected by the nation of Israel. They did not realise that as they saw the Lord going about, doing good (see Acts 10:38); and that they were watching God Himself at work in His creation. They completely misunderstood what the work of God entailed. So in John 3:19, we read:

> "And this is the condemnation, that the light has come into the world, and men loved darkness rather than light, because their deeds were evil."

Mankind does not want the light of God to shine in this world for it reveals just how far they are from pleasing God. Like a beetle scurrying for cover when a rock is turned, so mankind would rather stay in the dark for shame of their deeds being revealed. Hardly a flattering summary of the glory of mankind but one that is necessary if we are going to do anything useful to improve the situation. So the question before us, then, is how can we in our day, or the psalmist writing maybe in about 1,000 B.C., move out of the darkness and live a life that is pleasing to God? Is it possible for us to know what God wants for our lives?

The first verse of this stanza, verse 105, is possibly the most well-known part of Psalm 119. We need to remind ourselves that psalms are Hebrew poetry. They are not direct teaching where every word has specific meaning. Unlike English poetry, which certainly used to use rhyme and metre as a way of being memorable and conveying its thoughts, Hebrew poetry uses repetition of thought. Sometimes this repetition of thought would use a strong contrast between two opposites. At other times, the psalmist would repeat the same thought just using different words. Sometimes the repetition would add a further thought to enhance the first thought.

Verse 105: "Your word is a lamp to my feet, and a light to my path."

For the psalmist, this word would have been the Pentateuch, the first five books in our Old Testament. Christians have the full revealed Word of God, complete and in our own language in our Bible. This is a blessing of the highest order. Imagine if you were to go to church and the Bible was read to you in Hebrew and Greek, with no-one to translate! Imagine if there was no Bible at all! For many in this world they do not need to imagine this – it is a sad reality.

Today, we have the complete Word of God, which tells us who God is and what He has done. It shows us how God would have us behave – it is a lamp and a light. Much has been said about the difference between a lamp and a light:

1. Some would see in this the difference between near and distant illumination. His Word will show us how to behave in a particular situation as a lamp illuminates the area immediately around a person. It will also show us how we ought to plan our lives and the kinds of priorities we should have as we will make life changing decisions in the way that the sunlight illuminates the whole country, not just my locality.

2. Others would see in verse 105 a promise that His Word will be a guide for us night and day. During the night we might light a lamp to help us see but during the day we throw open the curtains and let the

sunlight in. His Word is good for us day and night and it is an excellent habit to get into reading His Word in the morning and in the evening. Of course, we all lead different lives and what suits one will not suit another. However, if we can make time every day to read and think about His Word then we will be much helped in life.

3. Others would suggest that the lamp shows us where we are, and the light shows us where we need to go. In that respect, His Word not only exposes the failures and problems in our life but also shows us what we need to do about them.

Undoubtedly, all these three things are true of the Word of God, although they may not necessarily have been in the mind of the psalmist as he wrote these words. In a day when we hear so much about relative truth and self-perception, it is good to know that God has given us *absolute* truth and has not only revealed to us all we need to know about Him, but also all we need to know in order to live a life that is pleasing to Him.

Verse 106: "I have sworn and confirmed that I will keep Your righteous judgments."

It is so important to be settled in our minds of the course that our lives will take. We cannot know every circumstance that we will pass through. Very often we may feel like we are responding to events rather than deciding upon our own path. For sure, there will be times in life that we feel spiritually close to God. At other times we may feel spiritually down and quite distant from God. However, through thick and thin, we need to have made that conscious decision that at all times His Word will be the final authority in our lives and that it will be the principal voice that guides our every decision. Paul wrote to the Christians in Rome:

> "I beseech you therefore, brethren, by the mercies of God, that you present your bodies a living sacrifice, holy, acceptable to God, which is your reasonable service" (Romans 12:1).

This is a once-and-for-all thing that we do. I think it matches the sentiment of the psalmist exactly, when he said that he had sworn to keep His righteous judgments. Have you consciously made the decision that Christ, through His Word, will rule in your life in everything, now and for the rest of your life? It is the best kind of life. But then Paul continued:

> "And do not be conformed to this world, but be transformed by the renewing of your mind, that you may prove what is that good and acceptable and perfect will of God" (Romans 12:2).

I think this has more to do with the many every-day decisions we make:

- I am not going to get angry when I am stuck in the traffic jam.
- I am not going to share that juicy gossip.
- I am going to make time to speak to my neighbour.

The life of the committed Christian ought to be radically different from that of the unbeliever and for the better (Psalm 119:106). I think the psalmist had this in mind when he spoke about confirming that he would keep His righteous judgments. We show the truth of His Word by living it out! But in case we think that living a life in obedience to His Word will mean that everything goes well and is a path to ease and comfort, verse 107 show us that the opposite is true.

Verse 107: "I am afflicted very much; revive me, O LORD, according to Your word."

Jesus promised His disciples:

> "Remember the word that I spoke to you,
> 'A servant is not greater than his master.'
> If they persecuted Me, they will also
> persecute you" (John 15:20).

There can be no doubt that this world rejected Him, and still does by and large. We cannot expect anything less, particularly when we live out the truth of His Word. It will not be a popular lifestyle. However, it will be one that may attract some to faith and we can be sure that, amidst the suffering, He will be present. The psalmist could elsewhere say:

> "He restores my soul" (Psalm 23:3).

God knows our frame and will not push us beyond what we are able to endure for Him.

Verse 108: "Accept, I pray, the freewill offerings of my mouth, O LORD, and teach me Your judgments."

Verse 108 shows us the positive experience a life of obedience to His Word brings. Yes, there may be times of persecution and suffering but there will also be times of positively enjoying Christ:

> "Therefore by Him let us continually
> offer the sacrifice of praise to God, that

is, the fruit of our lips, giving thanks to
His name" (Hebrews 13:15).

I still remember our children's head teacher praising her
children after a concert. Personally, I thought the music
had not been that good and the singing even worse. But
she really was encouraging them. When we praise God,
there is no chance that we will be saying anything that is
more than God deserves. It is simply not possible to
praise Him too much. The strange thing is, though, that
when we do praise Him, we so often feel so much the
better for it. I can recall frequently going to a Bible study
on a Friday evening, sometimes straight from work. At
the end of the week I was exhausted. However, after two
hours of study and then fellowship and singing I felt like
I could climb Everest! Praise is not only right for Him,
but it is good for us.

Neither was the psalmist happy with what he already
knew and so he prays "teach me Your judgments" (verse
108b), literally, "keep on teaching me Your judgments."
No matter whether we are a young Christian or one who
has been saved for many decades, we do so need to keep
a spirit within us that longs to keep on growing. We
should never be satisfied with what we already know but
long to know more. This is not so that we can impress
others with our vast knowledge but so that we can help
them and understand the glories of our great God better.

Verse 109: "My life is continually in my hand, yet I do not forget Your law."

Verse 109 shows us that the Spirit filled life is anything
but dull and routine. Twice already the phrase "my life is
in my hands" has been written. It was true of David, as
he faced the giant (1 Samuel 19:5); and it was true of Job

(Job 13:14-15). His Word will help us to rightly value our lives. For the unbeliever, this present life is all there is. No wonder they want to fill it with self-pleasing. After all, they think that when it is gone it is gone. Those of us who know that this is not true but have come to know the greatness of our God, know that this present life is not all there is. There are things more important than life itself. So we can take our lives in our hands without fear because we know that they are held by Him who is far greater than ourselves. This does not mean we are reckless and foolhardy. It simply means that we know that He has control of our lives and they only have worth when lived in obedience to Him. He may call us to quiet and peaceful normality. Or he may call us to real danger. Either way, we ought to be ready, like Aquila and Priscilla, to lay down our necks (see Romans 16:4) for the Gospel.

Verse 110: "The wicked have laid a snare for me, yet I have not strayed from Your precepts."

In verse 110, we are again reminded of the danger that we will face in life. Earlier in Psalm 119, the psalmist said:

> "The proud have dug pits for me, which is
> not according to Your law" (verse 85).

Temptation comes in all forms and sizes, and we can be sure that when we resolve to follow the life of obedience to His Word, then the devil will soon find ways to cause trouble. Wherever God is at work, the devil will be doing his worst in the vain attempt to frustrate the plans of God. I think the kind of snare the psalmist had in mind was one that would entangle his footsteps and bring him down. No wonder he needed the light of God's Word for his every step. His Word is well able to speak to us in every situation in which we find ourselves. Sometimes we may need to dig a little. At other times we may need to wait and allow the Holy Spirit to apply His Word in just the right way. We can be sure, though, that in Christ we have sufficient resource to be able to stand firm in every circumstance:

- We have His Word.
- We have the indwelling Holy Spirit.
- We have the fellowship of His people.

We do not lack for resources, but we ought to challenge ourselves as to what extent we make use of them. A soldier engaged in active service needs to ensure he is fully armed, and his equipment is in working order. We cannot be surprised if we do not know how to respond in a godly way in a particular circumstance if we have neglected the study of His Word. For those who are ready and willing, Paul would say:

> "Therefore, my beloved brethren, be steadfast, immovable, always abounding in the work of the Lord, knowing that your labour is not in vain in the Lord" (1 Corinthians 15:58).

No attack of the devil, no cunning attempt to compromise the saint of God by an unbeliever can be successful against the believer who is obediently depending upon God.

Verse 111: "Your testimonies I have taken as a heritage forever, for they are the rejoicing of my heart".

Perhaps you have been to a stately house. On display is some furniture or a painting that has been handed down from one generation to the next. It has been in the family for centuries. Sometimes, when I see such things, I think they are really horrible – they may be worth a lot, but I would never have them in my home! Sometimes it is good to throw away old things and get new. However, when we consider His Word this should not be the case. What the psalmist had learnt of God's Word he would treasure forever. Perhaps you can look back on the times in your past when you heard the truth of the Bible being taught. Are His promises as precious today as they were then? There is a movement within the church today to dilute what His Word has to say so that it is more palatable to those who are not saved – to want to make our Christianity fit in with the current culture and thus forgetting that what is considered suitable today, will be considered wrong in a future generation. This is not right. What we read in His Word has stood the test of time because it is true. It is true because it comes from the One who is the Truth! He does not lie (Titus 1:2) and He will not change (Malachi 3:6, Hebrews 13:8). Nor should we! We can and should embrace change where all that is at stake is our personal preference, our comfort zone. But when it comes to His Word, let us value our Christian heritage and the plain truth of His Word.

Verse 112: "I have inclined my heart to perform Your statutes forever, to the very end."

The word for "end" has at its heart the idea of reward. So the psalmist could be saying that with the end in view, with the reward in view, he would keep going and not give up. How sad, if having completed 22 miles of the marathon race, the athlete was to give up on the home straight! Alternatively, the psalmist might be saying that keeping His Word was an end in itself. The blessing that comes from obedience to His Word is reward enough.

THE IMPORTANCE OF GOD'S WORD

Both are true and should be just the kind of encouragement we need to live faithfully for Him, so long as He leaves us here. May we always live for Him with the light of His Word shining upon our pathway and thus bring glory to Him.

ס

15.   SAMECH – verses 113-120

Gordon D Kell

Introduction

SAMECH is the fifteenth letter in the Hebrew alphabet. The letter SAMECH has a circular shape and in Jewish thinking is associated with the support which has its source in the infinite power of God. Certainly, the thought of spiritual supports runs through this stanza of Psalm 119.

Verse 113: "I hate the double-minded, but I love Your law."

It is interesting that the stanza begins with what the psalmist hates and what he loves — with the thoughts of the mind. Thoughts lead to words and words lead to actions. It is vital as Christians we learn to discern between the thoughts which are damaging to ourselves and others and the thoughts which display the mind of Christ and result in blessing to ourselves and others. We need to control our thoughts. The psalmist writes about hating vain thoughts or double-mindedness and loving the Word of God which sanctifies our thinking. He writes with great clarity.

The psalmist constantly contrasts what is of God and what is not. In verse 113, he contrasts his hatred of doublemindedness with his love for God's law. Being "double minded" or, in Moffatt's translation, "half and half"[20], is to be unstable and always doubting the Word of God. He contrasts this unhappy condition with his love for the Word of God. God's Word was the psalmist's constant companion. He loved God's Word and lived by its teaching. And he always found in it that which fed and sustained him spiritually and guided him practically.

Paul writes in Colossians:

> "If then you were raised with Christ, seek those things which are above, where Christ is, sitting at the right hand of God. Set your mind on things above, not on things on the earth. ...Therefore put to death your members which are on the earth: fornication, uncleanness, passion, evil desire, and covetousness, which is idolatry. Because of these things the wrath of God is coming upon the sons of disobedience, in which you yourselves once walked when you lived in them. But now you yourselves are to put off all these: anger, wrath, malice, blasphemy, filthy language out of your mouth. Do not lie to one another, since you have put off the old man with his deeds, and have put on the new man who is renewed in

[20] James Moffatt, *The Old Testament: a New Translation*, Volume 2, page 768, New York: George H. Doran Company, 1924.

knowledge according to the image of Him who created him" (Colossians 3:1-2, 5-10).

Paul also encourages us, in Philippians 2:5-11, to have the mind of Christ; and in 2 Corinthians 10:5 that "every thought may be brought into captivity to the obedience of Christ."

The world struggles to influence our thinking in all kinds of directions, but God appeals to us through His mercies, as in Romans 12:1-2:

> "I beseech you therefore, brethren, by the mercies of God, that you present your bodies a living sacrifice, holy, acceptable to God, which is your reasonable service. And do not be conformed to this world, but be transformed by the renewing of your mind, that you may prove what is that good and acceptable and perfect will of God."

James gives us an insight into the character and dangers of doublemindedness:

- "If any of you lacks wisdom, let him ask of God, who gives to all liberally and without reproach, and it will be given to him. But let him ask in faith, with no doubting, for he who doubts is like a wave of the sea driven and tossed by the wind. For let not that man suppose that he will receive anything from the Lord; he is a double-minded man, unstable in all his ways" (James 1:5-8).
- "Come near to God and he will come near to you. Wash your hands, you sinners, and purify your hearts, you double-minded" (James 4:8, NIV).

175

Verse 114: "You are my hiding place and my shield; I hope in Your word."

After describing his love for God's Word in verse 113, the psalmist describes God as his hiding place and his shield. This is a reference to the support and protection God gives and the way His Word sustains us spiritually:

> "You are my hiding place; You shall preserve me from trouble; You shall surround me with songs of deliverance. Selah" (Psalm 32:7).

A hiding place is a secret safe place. It brings to mind the wings of an eagle referred to by Boaz:

> "The LORD repay your work, and a full reward be given you by the LORD God of Israel, under whose wings you have come for refuge" (Ruth 2:12).

The Lord Jesus uses a similar illustration:

> "O Jerusalem, Jerusalem, the one who kills the prophets and stones those who are sent to her! How often I wanted to gather your children together, as a hen gathers her chicks under her wings, but you were not willing!" (Matthew 23:37).

These are places of safety and free from conflict. The shield, however, is needed for conflict. It is designed for battle. It protects, defends, and defeats the attacks of the enemy, as in Ephesians 6:16, "above all, taking the shield of faith with which you will be able to quench all the fiery darts of the wicked one." Paul was probably thinking of the Roman shield, which protected the whole body. When it was joined with the shields of other soldiers it provided

176

all-round protection for a group of soldiers. It is not simply that we have faith, but we are part of a fellowship of faith.

God is also our hiding place and shield. We can rely on his safekeeping through difficult times and the peace of His presence. But we also need to have a daily trust in God. We have a faith which protects us from spiritual and moral attacks.

The psalmist also expressed a *hope* in God's Word (verse 114b). In verses 113-114, the psalmist brings before us a *love* for the Word of God, *faith* in God as His hiding place and shield, and certain hope in the promises the Word of God gives. This hope looks at these promises as present and future certainties. In New Testament language hope is described as "an anchor for the soul" (see Hebrews 6:19).

These three thoughts of the hiding place, the shield and the hope remind us of the three vital aspects of our relationship with God through Christ. These are *love, faith, and hope*. His love keeps us safe; our faith proves His faithfulness, and our hope is a future certainty.

Verse 115: "Depart from me, you evildoers, for I will keep the commandments of my God!"

Verse 115 expresses the essence of Psalm 1:1, which is all about separation from the company of evildoers:

> "Blessed is the man who walks not in the counsel of the ungodly, nor stands in the path of sinners, nor sits in the seat of the scornful."

There is no basis of fellowship between the child of God and what is ungodly, sinful, and scornful. We have to make sure we are walking with, standing by, and sitting in the right company.

Psalm 1:2-3 express a delight in God's Word, the blessing it brings and fruitfulness it produces:

> "But his delight is in the law of the LORD,
> and in His law he meditates day and night.
> He shall be like a tree planted by the rivers
> of water, that brings forth its fruit in its
> season, whose leaf also shall not wither;
> and whatever he does shall prosper"
> (Psalm 1:2-3).

Psalm 1 ends with the judgment of the ungodly and the value God places on his people:

> "The ungodly are not so, but are like the
> chaff which the wind drives away.
> Therefore the ungodly shall not stand in
> the judgment, nor sinners in the
> congregation of the righteous. For the
> LORD knows the way of the righteous, but
> the way of the ungodly shall perish"
> (Psalm 1:4-6).

Psalm 1 presents the godly man as someone who walks faithfully before God and finds all his resources in the presence of God. These themes are also found in this stanza of Psalm 119 (verses 113-120).

Verse 116: "Uphold me according to Your word, that I may live; and do not let me be ashamed of my hope."

Verse 116 continues the psalmist's thoughts about the importance of dependence upon God. The psalmist is upheld by the promises of God declared in His Word.

These promises are fulfilled in the lives of those who walk humbly before their God (see Micah 6:8). The psalmist trusts God to be faithful to His own Word. He appeals to God to uphold him so that he can continue to live for God. He prays that he might live in a way which witnesses to the faithfulness of God.

Again, the psalmist uses the word, "hope". His hope was in God. He did not want his life to be inconsistent with his hope. He knew God would not fail but the psalmist was concerned about his own failure. Sometimes we feel like this. We truly believe in God's faithfulness, but we are concerned about our own frailties. We should always be aware of our weakness but never cease to have confidence in our God. In the New Testament, hope is presented as a future certainty. This is different to the way we often use the word. In everyday speech we use hope to describe uncertainty. It may happen, it may not.

The writer of Hebrews describes it in this way:

> "We have this hope as an anchor for the soul, firm and secure, It enters the inner sanctuary behind the curtain" (Hebrews 6:19, NIV).

John writes:

> "Beloved, now we are children of God; and it has not yet been revealed what we shall be, but we know that when He is revealed, we shall be like Him, for we shall see Him as He is. And everyone who has this hope in Him purifies himself, just as He is pure" (1 John 3:2-3).

Our hope is in Christ. It is a transforming hope which should change us into His likeness.

Verse 117: "Hold me up, and I shall be safe, and I shall observe Your statutes continually."

Although the psalmist did not have the New Testament revelation of the Christian's hope, he nevertheless prays for God's strength to enable him to live a consistent life of faith. In his first appeal to God to uphold him he was thinking of the power this would give him to live for God. In the second appeal he sees that God's power to uphold him brings security and the opportunity to witness to God through his obedience:

> "I shall observe Your statutes continually"
> (verse 117b).

"Statutes" literally mean "things inscribed". It conveys a sense of permanence, and it teaches us about the eternal character of God's Word – it does not pass away. Jesus said:

> "Heaven and earth will pass away, but My words will by no means pass away" (Matthew 24:35).

The psalmist expresses his dependence upon God and he also expresses his understanding that his life and its value as a witness to God rests entirely upon the sustaining power of God. This is a reminder of what Jesus explains to us:

> "I am the vine, you are the branches. He who abides in Me, and I in him, bears much fruit; for without Me you can do nothing" (John 15:5).

Verse 118: "You reject all those who stray from Your statutes, for their deceit is falsehood."

In contrast with walking in dependence upon God, the Psalmist highlights God's judgment of those who turn away from His Word and also exposes their deceitful character. The psalmist desires to keep close to God and to draw on God's sustaining power in order to live for Him. But he also wisely observes the pattern of life of those who have turned away from God and the deceit which marks their lives. They expected God's blessing but lived lives of disobedience. The psalmist teaches us on the one hand to stay close to the Saviour whilst at the same time to beware of being drawn into a pattern of life based on the rejection of God and His claims upon us.

Verse 119: "You put away all the wicked of the earth like dross; therefore I love Your testimonies."

In verse 119, the psalmist views the judgment of God upon the wicked. He looks on to God's perfect judgment and the day when He will act in complete righteousness and justice. In contrast he loves God's testimonies and promises they give of God's present and future blessings.

Verse 120: "My flesh trembles for fear of You, and I am afraid of Your judgment."

The psalmist has a vivid sense of the greatness and holiness of God. He was also afraid of God's judgment.

It is only when we come to the New Testament that we understand that God has done everything to meet all His holy requirements so that we can become His children. He did this at His own cost through His Son Jesus Christ. Jesus Christ answered all our need at the Cross of Calvary when in love He took our place. Through faith in the Lord Jesus Christ we learn His love has made it possible for us to know peace with God (Romans 5:1), the peace of God (Philippians 4:7) and the God of peace (Hebrews 13:20). As a result of our faith in Him we do not tremble nor are we afraid because through Christ, and in the words of another psalm:

> "Mercy and truth have met together;
> righteousness and peace have kissed"
> (Psalm 85:10).

Let us rejoice in Christ's love, obey His Word, and seek to worship, follow, and serve our Saviour.

ע

16.   AYIN – verses 121-128

Yannick Ford

Introduction

Verses 121-128, all begin with the Hebrew letter AYIN. It apparently has the meaning of eye.

It was stated in the Introduction to this book that Psalm 119 is a sort of celebration of God's Word. Interestingly, the first two verses in this stanza, particularly verse 122, appear to be some of the very few verses of Psalm 119 that do not directly mention the Word of God in some form or other. However, they do refer to it, or at least allude to it. Indeed, by considering Psalm 119 as a celebration of God's Word, an understanding can be gained of this otherwise seemingly difficult-to-apply stanza.

Verse 121: "I have done justice and righteousness; do not leave me to my oppressors."

The psalmist starts off this stanza by saying:

> "I have done justice and righteousness"
> (verse 121a).

Where would he have found the instructions and directions for doing justice and righteousness? What are justice and righteousness, in any case? Are they just the general opinion of the times that we happen to live in? The psalmist would have found his instructions for justice and righteousness *in the Word of God*. In the Old Testament, a great importance was placed on both knowing and doing according to the Word of God. For example, Joshua was told:

> "This Book of the Law shall not depart from your mouth, but you shall meditate in it day and night, that you may observe to do according to all that is written in it. For then you will make your way prosperous, and then you will have good success" (Joshua 1:8).

Joshua had a great task in front of him. He was responsible for leading the whole nation of Israel as the next leader of the people after Moses. God told him that by meditating on and following His Word, Joshua would be successful in the task that had been given to him.

The same spirit governed the requirements for Israel's king. In Deuteronomy 17:18-20, instructions were given for when Israel would later have a king, specifically what the king was to do:

"Also it shall be, when he sits on the throne of his kingdom, that he shall write for himself a copy of this law in a book, from the one before the priests, the Levites. And it shall be with him, and he shall read it all the days of his life, that he may learn to fear the LORD his God and be careful to observe all the words of this law and these statutes, that his heart may not be lifted above his brethren, that he may not turn aside from the commandment to the right hand or to the left, and that he may prolong his days in his kingdom, he and his children in the midst of Israel."

The king was to copy out God's Word, and to read it daily, so that he could be successful as a ruler, and be a blessing to his people. You can see that if you had to write out the Word for yourself, and then read it every day, how it would become well grafted in as a part of your life.

In summary, what we can see from these quotes, from Joshua and from Deuteronomy, is that *the Word of God* was to be the rule of life. No doubt the writer of Psalm 119 had likewise been studying the Word of God, so that he could say:

"I have done justice and righteousness" (verse 121a).

But the Word that he had been studying was not just a dead book, like a dry set of archaic precepts and commands. It was the Word of the Living God. That is why, having followed God's Word, he was then able ask the Author of the Word to protect him:

"Do not leave me to my oppressors"
(verse 121b).

Verse 122: Be surety for Your servant for good; do not let the proud oppress me."

Furthermore, he was counting on the Author of the Word to make good His promises and to come in for him, to answer for him, and to take up his cause:

> "Be surety for Your servant for good; do not let the proud oppress me" (verse 122).

This dynamic interaction between the Word itself and the Author of the Word is most interesting. It shows us someone who is reading and studying God's Word, and then asking God to act according to it. In other words, he is praying back God's Word to God! It is not so much simple reading but rather a kind of conversation; and it has an application for us in New Testament times. For instance, we put our trust in God's Word, because we recognise that it is evidently a revelation from God. Even as the Word reveals God to us, we find by experience that what it says about God is indeed true. This then helps us to put our faith in God's Word for important, fundamental matters where we must trust what He says to us, because no other source can enlighten us (such as what happens to us after death, and how we can be sure of our eternal destiny). This also applies to the small details of life. In every case we can have a conversation with God as we see how the Word of God applies to our circumstances, and we can ask God to act according to what He has revealed and promised in His Word.

The psalmist wanted God to be a surety for him for good – in other words, for God to fully take up his case, and to vindicate him before his enemies. A surety is a guarantee, or security, but since we are talking about a personal God, we can rather say that He is the Guarantor. The psalmist wanted God to deliver him from the proud boasts and accusations of his oppressors, whoever they were. In a much greater sense, we trust that the Lord Jesus is indeed our Surety for all that concerns our forgiveness, redemption, and blessing. Thankfully, this is actually true because we are told that:

> "Jesus has become a surety of a better covenant" (Hebrews 7:22).

There we have it, in black and white, that He is our Surety, our Guarantor. Whatever we lacked, He supplied. He took our sin upon Himself, and we had His righteousness imputed to us, as we can read and understand when we go through the epistle to the Romans. Knowing that He is our Surety, we can trust Him for the future, and particularly for His promises regarding our ultimate destiny. If we know that the Word of God is true and reliable, then we can happily trust in such words of the Lord Jesus as these:

> "Most assuredly, I say to you, he who hears My word and believes in Him who sent Me has everlasting life, and shall not come into judgment, but has passed from death into life" (John 5:24).

If we did not know the Person who had said such things, it would seem rash to stake our eternal destiny and our present manner of life on such a statement. But we do know Him, and we can be sure that what He says is true!

Verses 123-124: "My eyes fail from seeking Your salvation and Your righteous word. Deal with Your servant according to Your mercy, and teach me Your statutes."

The dynamic interaction between the Word and its Author continues in verses 123-124. The psalmist's eyes fail for seeking God's salvation and God's righteous Word. I think that means he wants to see the salvation, or deliverance, from his problem *in God's Word*; and he wants to see that salvation in practice. He understands that, even if he can say, "I have done justice and righteousness" (verse 121a), nevertheless he still needs God's mercy, and he needs God to keep on teaching him, hence he continues:

> "Deal with Your servant according to Your mercy, and teach me Your statutes" (verse 124).

We express a similar sentiment in our New Testament times. Like the psalmist, we continually depend upon God's grace. In his book *We Would see Jesus*[21], Roy Hession explains that Paul's epistles are full of the phrase 'through Jesus Christ our Lord,' and that so often Paul does not mention blessings without immediately adding, 'through Jesus Christ our Lord.' It is certainly true that all of our blessings, both current and future, are according to God's grace. No doubt this is why, the apostle Paul told Timothy:

> "You therefore, my son, be strong in the grace that is in Christ Jesus" (2 Timothy 2:1).

[21] Roy Hession, *We Would See Jesus*, CLC Publications, 1978.

Indeed, the very last verse of the Bible says:

> "The grace of our Lord Jesus Christ be
> with you all. Amen" (Revelation 22:21).

We need God's grace, just as the psalmist realised that he needed God's mercy.

We also need to be taught, just as the psalmist requested God to teach him His statutes. Again Paul instructed Timothy:

> "Consider what I say, and may the Lord
> give you understanding in all things"
> (2 Timothy 2:7).

This need for understanding is a very important aspect of the dynamic interaction between us, God's Word, and God Himself.

Verse 125: "I am Your servant; give me understanding, that I may know Your testimonies."

In the final four verses of this stanza, we read that the psalmist is asking for help to cling to God's Word in a time when it is generally disregarded. He starts off by requesting understanding in verse 125:

> "I am Your servant; give me
> understanding, that I may know Your
> testimonies."

Largely speaking, the Bible is not a particularly difficult book to read. Faithful, easy-to-read translations are available. It is true that there are some sections, for example in the prophets, that are not necessarily simple to interpret, but on the whole, the actual message of the Bible is pretty simple. (It is not like some poetry classes that I still remember from school when I could not make much sense of the text!) However, without the enlightenment of the Holy Spirit, the Bible will remain a dead book to us, as Paul says:

> "These things we also speak, not in words which man's wisdom teaches but which the Holy Spirit teaches, comparing spiritual things with spiritual. But the natural man does not receive the things of the Spirit of God, for they are foolishness to him; nor can he know them, because they are spiritually discerned" (1 Corinthians 2:13-14).

The actual text of the Bible is simple enough, but for it to really mean something for us, for it to transform us, we need the understanding of the Holy Spirit. Now this is not a mystical or esoteric thing that we somehow need to attain to by our own efforts, but rather it is simply allowing the Word of God to speak to our conscience. The Holy Spirit is more than willing to make good His message to us, if we will let Him. That is why the apostle says three times in Hebrews chapters 3 and 4:

> "Today, if you will hear His voice, do not harden your hearts."

God wants us to hear His message, so He will not make it difficult for us to hear it, but we can block it out by hardening our hearts.

Verse 126: "It is time for You to act, O LORD, for they have regarded Your law as void."

One of the reasons that the Psalmist wanted understanding, was so that he could properly apply God's Word, because he lived in a day when it was disregarded.

Since we do not know who the human author of Psalm 119 was, we cannot fix it to a particular time in Israel's history. But that does not really matter, as we can see how the principles in that psalm are generally applicable. It would be easy enough, in one sense, to follow God's Word if that was what everyone else around us was doing. But what if God's Word is unpopular, distrusted, and considered as being of no relevance? That seemed to be the case for the psalmist, since he says:

> "They have regarded Your law as void"
> (verse 126b).

In such a case we need understanding to be able to wisely apply God's Word in our own lives and circumstances, and we need to see the encouragement of God acting in our lives according to His Word, which strengthens us in our trust and obedience. How does God do this for us? I think we have a clue in the final two verses – God helps us by giving us a love for His Word, and an understanding that His Word is indeed true and right.

Verses 127-128: "Therefore I love Your commandments more than gold, yes, than fine gold! Therefore all Your precepts concerning all things I consider to be right; I hate every false way."

If we do not love something, we are unlikely to want to be involved with it, particularly if circumstances are against it anyway. That was the situation with the psalmist:

> "They have regarded Your law as void"
> (verse 126b).

It would have been easier for him to also walk away from that law. But he loved God's Word:

"I love Your commandments more than
gold, yes, than fine gold!"(verse 127).

As to why he loved God's Word, we can find out by other
verses within the whole of Psalm 119. Here are a few
examples:

- "My soul melts from heaviness; strengthen me
  according to Your word" (verse 28). The psalmist
  had found that God's Word had strengthened him
  when he was depressed.

- "Let Your mercies come also to me, O LORD –
  Your salvation according to Your word" (verse 41).
  The psalmist had found deliverance through God's
  Word.

- "Remember the word to Your servant, upon which
  You have caused me to hope. This is my comfort in
  my affliction, For Your word has given me life"
  (verses 49-50). The Word of God had given life to
  the psalmist, and he staked his hope upon it.

- "You have dealt well with Your servant, O LORD,
  according to Your word" (verse 65).

- "Your word is a lamp to my feet and a light to my
  path" (verse 105). No wonder he loved this Word!

Since the psalmist loved God's Word, he was prepared to
stick to it, even if it was generally disregarded. He was not
going to throw away something that had given him life,
hope and direction. We can see how this can apply to us
today.

192

The psalmist was also convinced that God's Word was right:

> "Therefore all Your precepts concerning all things I consider to be right; I hate every false way" (verse 128).

If we think that God's Word is wrong, and inappropriate, we will not be inclined to keep it. But if we go back to verse 121b, "I have done justice and righteousness," we remember that the very concepts of justice and righteousness are within God's Word. God's Word reveals the just and righteous God. Consequently, we trust His precepts. We know that what He says is right, as verse 160 states:

> "The entirety of Your word is truth, and every one of Your righteous judgments endures forever."

It is an incredibly bold claim, as its scope extends to the whole of the Word for the whole of time!

Conclusion

This then is the message of this stanza (verses 121-128) of Psalm 119 – a dynamic interaction between the reader, God's Word, and God Himself, which is a kind of conversation where we pray back God's Word to God. I must confess, when I first considered this stanza to prepare the original talk for *Truth for Today,* I wondered how I would approach it and what spiritual food I would derive from it. It seemed like a difficult passage to gain encouragement from, and it reminded me of Spurgeon's comments about Psalm 119 that are quoted in the Introduction to this book. However, Spurgeon ended up being pleased by having expended "pleasurable toil" in studying Psalm 119. In the same way, I have gained blessing in thinking about how verses 121-128 set out the value of God's Word, and I trust you will have been blessed too.

פ

17. PEH – verses 129-136

Jonathan Hughes

Introduction

Consider these three quotes:

1. 'It is a far, far better thing that I do, than I have ever done; it is a far, far better rest that I go to than I have ever known' (Charles Dickens, *A Tale of Two Cities*).

2. 'I know I have the body but of a weak and feeble woman; but I have the heart and stomach of a king, and of a king of England too, and think foul scorn that Parma or Spain, or any prince of Europe, should dare to invade the borders of my realm: to which rather than any dishonour shall grow by me, I myself will take up arms, I myself will be your general, judge, and rewarder of every one of your virtues in the field' (Elizabeth 1, *Tilbury speech*).

3. 'You ask, what is our aim? I can answer in one word: Victory. Victory at all costs—Victory in spite of all terror—Victory, however long and hard the road may be, for without victory there is no survival. I have nothing to offer but blood, toil, tears and

sweat' (Winston Churchill, *House of Commons, May 13, 1940*).

Words matter. These three quotes show how stirring the use of language can be. They show us the power that lies behind our words.

The whole of Psalm 119 speaks about the Psalmist's delight in the Word of God. This stanza is no different, although each verse has a slightly different emphasis. Perhaps though, before we consider what the verses say we do need to ask ourselves the question: 'What value do I put on the Bible, the inspired Word of God?' I do not know if you have ever watched a quiz programme on television. The contestants may be really clever and know a lot about all sorts of things but whenever there is a question on Bible knowledge, even the simple things prove beyond the knowledge of most contestants. The level of Bible knowledge in society today is shockingly bad and this is having catastrophic consequences. If we do not appreciate that humanity is unique, created in God's image, then we can hardly be surprised when we do not treat one another in the way that God expects us to. It is only in the Bible that we can find out why we are unique and have worth. Now you might say that the Bible is a really important book – that is good. I might say that I love my wife, but if I am never at home, and ignore her needs and aspirations then you might rightly question the quality of my love and the truthfulness of my words! So let me ask you again: 'What value do you put upon the Word of God?' It ought to form the basis of every aspect of our lives. Normal Christianity is entirely based upon daily Bible study. It is abnormal and wrong to claim to be a Christian and not to want to let God's Word have

196

control over every aspect of life. We can only do this by reading it and understanding what it has to say.

Verse 129: "Your testimonies are wonderful; therefore my soul keeps them."

The Psalmist begins his meditation in this stanza with the words:

> "Your testimonies are wonderful" (verse 129a).

What a great start! The Psalmist repeats the thought from verse 18 that God's Word is "wonderful". It is also the same word that Isaiah uses to describe the person of the Lord Jesus:

> "For unto us a Child is born, unto us a Son is given; and the government will be upon His shoulder. And His name shall be called Wonderful" (Isaiah 9:6).

In God's eyes, there is no difference between the written word of God and the second Person of the Godhead, the living incarnate Word of God. John reinforces this theme in the introduction to his Gospel:

> "In the beginning was the Word, and the Word was with God, and the Word was God. … And the Word became flesh and dwelt among us" (John 1:1, 14).

It is absolutely vital that I have this clearly in my mind:

> "Jesus Christ is the same yesterday and today and forever" (Hebrews 13:8).

And so the Bible is also unchangeable. Jesus Christ showed us what God the Father is like and so does the

Bible. Jesus Christ was perfect and so is the Bible. Jesus Christ came that we might have life and the Bible is full of life-giving words. The two stand or fall together, but what we cannot do is claim to love Jesus but think that the Bible is out-of-date or bits of it do not have something to say to us anymore. No wonder the Psalmist could then say:

> "Therefore my soul keeps them" (verse 129b).

If Jesus were physically in the room with me, I would never dream of telling a lie to you in His hearing. If He were in the car then I would not want Him to hear me fume at other road users. So why do I treat the Bible, and therefore Him, with such disrespect?

Verse 130: "The entrance of Your words gives light; it gives understanding to the simple."

Generally, houses at that time had only one door and no windows. So other than lighting a lamp, the only way that light could enter a home was through the door. The Psalmist is telling us that the Bible is the door through which the light of God can shine into the house of our lives. Of course, if the door were kept shut then the inside of the house would have no natural light. So Jesus would say:

> "Behold, I stand at the door and knock. If anyone hears My voice and opens the door, I will come in to him" (Revelation 3:20).

Our lives need to be wide open to the Bible and all that it has to teach us so that we can fully enjoy the warmth and light of the presence of God. This is not a mystical experience. It is something that is achieved through the regular and systematic study of the Bible. Only as I allow His Word to dictate my actions in every aspect of my life can I experience the light of God. Perhaps, using this picture, you will see what happens when we only allow God into a small part of our lives. We may serve Him on Sunday, but feel that is sufficient; after all, we do not want to be a fanatic! But that is like only opening the door ajar. No sane person would want to live in the gloomy cold when the full light and warmth of the sun was available!

The effect of living in the light of God routinely is that it gives understanding. I do not want to say that there may never be perplexing and difficult days for saints of God who daily expose their lives to the light of God's Word. However, I do need to question myself as to whether the reason so often I do not really understand what God is doing or why He has allowed such and such to happen is because His light had not brought understanding. Now this cannot be a fault of God so it must be because I have not opened the door wide to Him. Perhaps next time I find myself questioning God, I need carefully to look and see whether I have become lazy in my Bible study!

Verse 131: "I opened my mouth and panted, for I longed for Your commandments."

This verse really speaks about our attitude to God's Word. There is a connection to Psalm 42:1:

> "As the deer pants for the water brooks,
> so pants my soul for You, O God."

This world is a spiritually dry place and as we go to work and as we spend our leisure time, we are going to become spiritually dry too. Time spent in His Word and in His company is like water to a thirsty animal, without which it would soon die. Perhaps, the metaphor is of an animal pursued by ferocious predators to the point of exhaustion, panting in great gulps of oxygen to strengthen muscles required for safety. Or perhaps the metaphor is of a new-born baby yelling because it is hungry, desperate for its next meal. So Peter could write:

> "As new-born babes, desire the pure milk
> of the word, that you may grow thereby"
> (1 Peter 2:2).

I can remember when our children were small, them giving a good yell and going bright red in the face, but as soon as the milk arrived all was well! That child was not going to be distracted or put off until it was fed. What a challenge to me as to how much I really desire His Word. Too often, I am too tired to study, or I do not feel like it, or I am too busy. So many excuses not to feed myself with His Word and none of them will do me any good. If we are serious about wanting to grow in our Christian lives and so become more like the Lord Jesus, which should be our natural desire, then we need to feed on His Word. There are no short cuts to growth. There is a divine feast waiting for me between the covers of my Bible. However, it will do me no good whatsoever whilst it stays there! I need to read His Word and study it with all the intellect that God has given me. I then need to apply it to my life and refresh my often-faulty memory so that it is constantly on my mind. Perhaps then, this confusing life will start to make a whole lot more sense as I learn to view things with my God's eyes.

Verse 132: "Look upon me and be merciful to me, as Your custom is toward those who love Your name."

The Psalmist's heartfelt plea is that God would look at Him in mercy. The Hebrew word for 'look' is translated as 'turn' in other places. I think that the Psalmist has in mind that he knows he is a sinful man, and that God finds his sin abhorrent. Yet he longs that God will turn towards him and restore him. I think we have a lovely example of this in the life of the Lord Jesus Himself. In Luke's Gospel, after Peter had three times denied the Lord Jesus, we read:

> "And the Lord turned and looked at Peter. And Peter remembered the word of the Lord. …So Peter went out and wept bitterly" (22:61-62).

In the Psalmist's mind there would be nothing worse than God turning away from him permanently with no hope for the future. For Peter this must have been an excruciating look, one that shook him to the very core. Yet it was also the look that started his restoration – full of mercy and pity. It is at times when we realise that we have failed God that we most need to get back into His presence. We might feel that we do not belong there or that we have sinned too much to be forgiven. The devil will do his utmost to keep us away from God. We, like the Psalmist, and like Peter, need that look from the Lord Jesus. It is a look that acknowledges who we are and what we have done, but a look that will also lead us to realise that we are frankly forgiven. I remember listening to the parents of a suicide bomber saying that they cannot even look at a picture of their son now – it is just too painful.

Oh, the wonderful mercy of God that He always looks upon us and wants to restore us to a full and close relationship with Him!

Verse 133: "Direct my steps by Your word, and let no iniquity have dominion over me."

In verses 131-132, we thought about the Psalmist's attitude and plea. In verse 133, we see his walk. We have seen already that, in one sense, it is good to be like a baby with a powerful desire for the milk of the Word. However, this verse goes on to show that spiritual growth is expected in the life of the Christian. "Direct [or, order] my steps" speaks about them having a purpose. We are not to be spiritual toddlers spending as much time on our backside as we do on our feet. Nor are we to stagger about unsure as to whether our legs will keep us up, like a drunkard. Our spiritual walk, our manner of life, is to be purposeful and divinely directed. There is a goal to be reached and each step that we take, each action that we make, should be in a straight line towards that goal. Like a snare, sin lurks waiting to trip us up and hinder our spiritual walk. How very much we need His Word to protect us!

Paul in writing to the Christians in Ephesus 6, describes the Bible as the sword of the Spirit. There is no greater defence for the believer than allowing the Holy Spirit to take what we have read in our daily quiet time and bring it to mind throughout the day. Here we see the wonderful partnership that we have in God's work. It is our responsibility to fill our minds with His Word. It is His responsibility to actively apply that to every situation we face and to produce Christ honouring behaviour in our lives. Can we imagine soldiers going into battle only to realise they have forgotten to bring their weapons with them? How foolish an oversight. And yet, how many times do we try to go through a day without equipping ourselves with the Spirit's sword – the Bible? The believer who walks closely to the Lord in the power of His Word will soon meet opposition. This is the subject of verse 134.

Verse 134: "Redeem me from the oppression of man, that I may keep Your precepts."

I think that in twenty-first century Britain one of the greatest oppositions that we face is that of despondency. We have tried to serve the Lord and it does not seem to achieve anything. We have preached the Gospel, and no one person is saved. We have tried to teach His Word and others just go their own way. Modern Christianity is so lukewarm that He is preparing to spew that religious world out of His mouth. Is there any point in carrying on the struggle?

As a young lad I loved reading the Ladybird series of books on historical characters. One that really had an impact was the story of Captain Scott. The selfless heroism of Captain Oates and the accomplishment of human endeavour were sure to fire the imagination of a young boy. However, I could never really understand why they entered their tent that last fateful time and never came out. After all, had they known it, they were so close to the next food dump compared to the hundreds of miles they had already covered. If only! We stand on the threshold of eternity and the Lord may come at any moment. Now is not the time for slack hands and weak knees. Now is the time for selflessness and energetic endeavour. If we only knew what lies just around the corner, just beyond the material horizon. The eternity that beckons is so vastly superior to anything that we have imagined. May we be inspired to keep His precepts and live out the truth of His Word in a lovely and welcoming display of real Christianity. Not for us the stuff that most play at – that fills a Sunday and ensures we have a suit in the wardrobe. His Word calls us to lay down our lives, to deny ourselves and to follow Him into our workplace, or the mission field, through thick and thin regardless of the cost!

Verse 135: "Make Your face shine upon Your servant, and teach me Your statutes."

For the one who overcomes we have the promise of untold glory. So the Psalmist continues his meditation on the Word by saying:

> "Make Your face shine upon Your servant" (verse 135a).

This sentiment echoes the priestly prayer of Aaron:

> "The LORD bless you and keep you; the LORD make His face shine upon you, and be gracious to you; the LORD lift up His countenance upon you, and give you peace" (Numbers 6:24-26).

What a lovely prayer – simple and beautiful! What an enormous privilege to have the face of God shining upon us. I believe that it is something that the Lord experienced in His own life as He was baptised. The heavens were opened, and the voice proclaimed the pleasure of God in His well-beloved Son. Here was a Man who deservedly lived in the sunshine of God's face. Jesus was the One who always did those things that pleased His Father. The pleasure of God was of utmost importance to the Lord Jesus in all things. I wonder, how much does the pleasure of God mean to me? Does it even matter at all? Perhaps you can remember back to your courting days when the pleasure of your partner was very much a matter of concern. It really mattered. Perhaps not so much now. How sad if we have really lost the desire to have the face of God shine upon us!

Still the Psalmist would learn more of God's Word. 135 verses into his psalm and his prayer continues to be:

> "Teach me Your statutes" (verse 135b).

No matter how long we have been a believer, no matter how long we have learnt from His Word, no matter how often we have read it through from cover to cover, we need to retain a teachable heart with a desire to learn more. In this life, the only things that do not grow are dead!

Verse 136: "Rivers of water run down from my eyes, because men do not keep Your law."

What a challenge to conclude this stanza with! Here the Psalmist displays a sensitivity of heart to the things of God. He was deeply upset about the moral condition of the society in which he lived. There was real anguish as he saw the sinfulness of those around him. Jesus Himself is the greatest example of this moral sensitivity:

> "Now as He drew near, He saw the city
> and wept over it" (Luke 19:41).

In John 11:35 we simply read, "Jesus wept." Sin and the resultant death had no place in His creation, it ought not to have been. There was a holy rage as well as a tender sympathy that brought the Lord to tears. He truly knew what it was to be a holy Man in an unholy world, and it hurt!

Sadly, today, so often my response may be a weary shrug of the shoulders as yet another Christian is accused of wrongdoing, or a 'Well, what do you expect from the lost?' as some sickening crime hits the news. That is simply not good enough. By spending time in His Word my conscience and moral sensitivity will be conformed to God's way of thinking and I will see wrong for what it truly is – an offence against God and rebellion against His authority. Surely then, I too will be deeply affected, maybe even to tears by the state of our society. God does not need any more judges – He has that task in hand. He does need those broken-hearted individuals who are ready to stand up against the moral decline of our age and graciously demonstrate how simple and complete obedience to His Word is just so much better in all ways and for all times. Are you such a person?

צ

18.   TSADDI – verses 137-144

PETER OLLERHEAD

Introduction

This stanza, verses 137 to 144, is the eighteenth of the twenty-two stanzas and is entitled, in some Bibles, as TSADDI. Unlike many of the psalms which are headed by the name of an author, such as Moses or David, Psalm 119 is anonymous – though Cheyne, in his study of the Psalms, suggests that it was written by an older man with, 'a rich and varied experience behind him; persecution and captivity have long been his portion, but he trusts in the salvation of Jehovah, and looks forward to witnessing for God before kings.'[22] Whether or not this is true, what is certain is the author's confidence and trust in God and His Law.

[22] Thomas Kelly Cheyne (1841-1915), *The Book of Psalms: or The Praises of Israel*, page 318, London: Keegan Paul, Trench & Co., 1888.

Verse 137: "Righteous are you, O LORD, and right are your rules" (ESV).

We cannot ignore the preceding verse if we want rightly to understand the reason for the psalmist's definite claim that God is righteous, as are His rules or judgments. Verse 136 states that streams of tears flow from the psalmist's eyes, because the people did not keep the law of God. It greatly concerned him when his people deliberately disobeyed the Lord. He knew in his heart that, as God was righteous, He required that those who claimed to believe in Him should not deliberately ignore His law. Notice also in verse 137, that God's Word and rules are what God is. God is righteous; therefore everything that emanates from Him is righteous, or as another has written: '... the law is a true transcript of that Divine righteousness.'[23] We are not meant to wobble around the moral universe seeking differing answers as to how God would have us live! He has given to us the moral law and instructions to enable us to live as He would wish and to walk a pathway that is pleasing to Him. This does not turn believers into automatons, for we have to work out how to express our faith in the society in which we live. When I was young, I was involved in *Youth for Christ*, which was established in the United Kingdom by Billy Graham some seventy years ago. Its motto was 'Anchored to the Rock: Geared to the Times.' The writer of the letter to the Hebrews knew something of the certainty and stability of our links with God:

> "So that by two unchangeable things, in which it is impossible for God to lie, we who have fled for refuge might have

[23] Alexander MacLaren, *The Expositor's Bible; The Psalms, Volume III,* CXIX, page 281, New York: A. C. Armstrong and Sons, 1894.

strong encouragement to hold fast to the hope set before us. We have this as a sure and steadfast anchor of the soul, a hope that enters into the inner place behind the curtain, where Jesus has gone as a forerunner on our behalf…" (Hebrews 6: 18-20, ESV).

If these words from the Hebrew epistle are strange to you, from personal experience I urge you to study this letter, as it brought me to a better understanding of the spiritual essence of Christianity.

If there was an anchor for the soul in the early days of Christianity, we must reckon it as true now, for God cannot change. Of course, if we do not accept Scripture as a revelation of God, from God, we can change our beliefs as often as we change our socks. I trust that all readers, by grace, have concluded that the Bible is the Word of God and believe in the eternal, immortal God: the God who was finally and fully revealed to us through His Son, Jesus of Nazareth. This means that all that was revealed to the psalmist has been revealed to us. What it does not mean is that our personal faith in and understanding of God never changes. As we move through the various experiences of life, our faith in the Lord must deepen and our knowledge of Him, as revealed in Scripture, must increase. Over the years, has our faith been deepened and our knowledge increased? The last words that the Apostle Peter wrote to his fellow Christians were:

"But grow in the grace and knowledge of our Lord and Saviour Jesus Christ. To him be the glory both now and to the day of eternity. Amen" (2 Peter 3:18, ESV).

Though Peter had a personal knowledge of the historical Jesus, and had witnessed the resurrected Christ, he still valued the written Word, which for him would be the Old Testament – including Psalm 119:

> "Since you have been born again, not of perishable seed but of imperishable, through the living and abiding word of God" (1 Peter 1:23, ESV).

Verse 138: "You have appointed your testimonies in righteousness and in all faithfulness" (ESV).

In verse 137, the word that the psalmist used for God's written Word was "rules", which The New International Version translates as "laws". In verse 138, he uses "testimonies". Whatever the word or synonym is used, we must consider it as the authoritative Word of God, which was the stance that the Apostle Peter took.

In this stanza of Psalm 119, the emphasis is on righteousness, which must impress upon us the importance of this in the sphere where God dominates our thinking. There is a tendency in most of us to live just inside the rules and regulations. If they can be bent to our convenience and advantage so be it. Before I started writing these comments, I read in a daily newspaper of the Queen inviting some guests to shelter in the Royal Tent during a heavy shower of rain. Sadly, she was disappointed to find that some of the gold-plated teaspoons were missing, when the cutlery was counted at the end of the day. Obviously, the erring guests had no intention of stealing when they entered the Palace grounds. Even though they were not habitual thieves, they could not resist the temptation of taking such souvenirs. If not a life-threatening misdemeanour or a major crime, it was still an unrighteous action. With our God, His testimonies and laws reflect His righteousness. The emphasis He puts on righteousness is not merely a matter for technical argument or discussion of theological words. I believe that it can affect our lives for the better. Isaiah was confident of this because he wrote:

> "And the effect of righteousness will be peace, and the result of righteousness, quietness and trust for ever" (Isaiah 32: 17, ESV).

The Apostle Paul takes up the theme of righteousness in his letter to the Romans:

> "But now the righteousness of God has been manifested apart from the law, although the Law and the Prophets bear witness to it – the righteousness of God through faith in Jesus Christ for all who believe. For there is no distinction: for all have sinned and fall short of the glory of God, and are justified by his grace as a gift, through the redemption that is in Christ Jesus" (Romans 3:21-24, ESV).

The miracle of God's grace and love has accomplished what nothing else could do:

> "For God has done what the law, weakened by the flesh, could not do. By sending his own Son in the likeness of sinful flesh and for sin, he condemned sin in the flesh, in order that the righteous

requirement of the law might be fulfilled
in us, who walk not according to the flesh
but according to the Spirit" (Romans 8:3-
4, ESV).

The greatest display of God's righteousness and love is
seen at Calvary.

Verse 139: "My zeal consumes me, because my foes forget your words" (ESV).

In verse 136, the psalmist was sorrowful, to the point of
tears, when he witnessed ignorance of, and disobedience
to, God's law. In verse 139, it was his regard for the Law
which caused him distress when others ignored it. Do we
have zeal for the things of God, so that we feel injured
when the cause of Christ is mocked? We should not feel
persecuted if the scoffing is aimed personally at us, for
the Lord said that as He had been treated so His followers
would be. We should, however, feel it when His Name is
mocked, and His sacrifice despised. Verses 140 and 141
repeat the same regard for God's Word that the very first
psalm highlights, when it states that the man who is
blessed delights in the law of the LORD and meditates on
it day and night (see Psalm 1:2).

Verses 140-141: "Your promise is well tried, and your servant loves it. I am small and despised, yet I do not forget your precepts" (ESV).

How different is the attitude of the person who loves the
promises of God, compared with those who forgot His
Word! How precious to read that the psalmist considers
the Word "well tried" or "pure" (King James Version),
and that he "loves it." There is a thought in the word
"pure" that suggests it has been refined. Over the years,

countless Christians have proved the preciousness of the Word of God. We are not being fed with fables and myths, rather that which builds up and increases our knowledge of God. When she was aged twenty-four, my mother lost a son aged twenty months. Many years later, at the cemetery where he was buried, she pointed to some words carved into the stonework above the mortuary chapel door, which read:

> "As one whom his mother comforteth, so
> will I comfort you" (Isaiah 66:13, KJV).

Her comments still remain with me: 'When we buried Derek those words meant something to me.' Time and time again grieving people have been helped by the Word of God energised into our lives by the power of the Holy Spirit:

> O may these hallowed pages be
> My ever dear delight!
> And still new beauties may I see,
> And still increasing light.
> Divine Instructor, gracious Lord,
> Be Thou for ever near;
> Teach me to love Thy sacred Word,
> And view my Saviour there.

Anne Steele 1716-1778

Do we love the Word of God? If we do, we shall regularly read and obey it. In our age, if we are not careful, the comments on Facebook, Twitter, or some other social media platform, will engage our attention and monopolise our time.

Some commentators use verse 141 to suggest that the writer of this psalm was young. But I feel the psalm is the product of a mature, spiritual mind; it is the consideration of one who has long walked with God. Such a walk does not make him proud, or lifted-up, for he is conscious that he is small. This is a facet that we need to emulate, for humility and a humble spirit are valued by God (see Isaiah 66:2).

Verse 142: "Your righteousness is righteous for ever, and your law is true" (ESV).

As already stated, the psalmist never wanders far from the theme of righteousness in this stanza, and he takes it up again in verse 142. Bishop Ellicott translated this verse slightly differently:

> "Thy righteousness is right for ever, and
> thy law is truth."[24]

This makes it easier to understand because it shows that God's standard of righteousness is an abiding one, even if the entire world rejects it. We all need to acknowledge the fact that God requires righteousness from each one of us:

> "O LORD, who shall sojourn in your tent? Who shall dwell on your holy hill? He who walks blamelessly and does what is right and speaks truth in his heart" (Psalm 15:1-2, ESV).

It must be plainly stated that our standard of righteousness never reaches that which God requires. Paul distinguishes between our righteousness of moral effort, which he terms the "righteousness of the law" or "his own righteousness" (see Philippians 3:9). In that

---

[24] A. S. Aglen in Charles John Ellicott, *An Old Testament Commentary for English Readers*, Volume IV, Psalms, CXIX, page 267, Cassell and Company: London, 1884.

verse, Paul talks of the righteousness from God, which is ours as a gift from God, through the sacrificial death of Christ. Are we still trying to work our way into God's good books, or have we received the gift of God's righteousness, which comes to all those who believe in Jesus, the Son of God? The glorious truth that God has provided this righteousness for sinners is the central message of the Gospel. Do we believe it? Do we live it? Do we preach it?

Verse 143: "Trouble and anguish have found me out, but your commandments are my delight" (ESV).

Verse 143 encloses the enigma of bad things afflicting good people. Sometimes we are apt to think Christians should be free of trials and tribulations. That such thoughts enter our minds is a device of the enemy of our souls. If God really loves us, we think, why have I lost my job, suffer with a severe illness, or lose a loved one? Satan seeks to reduce our faith to nil, so that we cease to believe. We live in a world where such adversities can affect anybody at any time. The psalmist suffered a deluge of troubles, which could have caused him to swerve aside from his godly path. However, as the verse affirms, he never ceases to delight in the living Word of God.

The people of Isaiah's time were going to face severe distress when the Babylonian army entered Judea, killing many and taking back others as slaves. Isaiah had to tell them that God was aware of their pain. They thought that God had forgotten them and that their circumstances were unknown to Him. Isaiah went on to remind them of a long-forgotten truth that we do well to remember:

"Have you not known? Have you not heard? The LORD is the everlasting God, the Creator of the ends of the earth. He does not faint or grow weary; his understanding is unsearchable. He gives power to the faint, and to him who has no might he increases strength" (Isaiah 40: 28-29, ESV).

So then, when the evil days come and the light fades, do not lose heart and claim that God has let you down. Our God neither slumbers nor sleeps, so let us have the attitude of the psalmist and continue to trust in the Lord and delight in His Word. Do not be like the people of Isaiah's day who said that God had forgotten them. God being aware of our sinful state, did not turn His back on us. Instead, so great was His love that He sent His only begotten Son to suffer, bleed, and die to bring salvation to us, thus enabling us to live in the power of the endless life.

Verse 144: "Your testimonies are righteous for ever; give me understanding that I may live" (ESV).

"Testimonies" is one of the synonyms for God's Law or Word. There is also a sense in which it bears witness to the one who speaks. A witness in a court of law swears to tell the truth. (We know that sometimes this is not always the case.) He, or she, should bear testimony to what they saw or knew. Verse 144 bears witness to the eternal God, whose righteous pronouncements reflect His righteousness, for He is a righteous God. They do not change with the intellectual fashions of the day. We Christians are definitely not obscurantists; we are not against enlightenment. We are, however, followers of the

God whose promises have been tested time and time again, sometimes in the most dreadful of circumstances.

Verse 144 is a prayer for understanding. The psalmist wants to tread further into the limitless knowledge of the God, who according to Paul is:

> "The blessed and only Sovereign, the King of kings and Lord of lords, who alone has immortality, who dwells in unapproachable light, whom no one has ever seen or can see. To him be honour and eternal dominion. Amen" (1 Timothy 6:15-16, ESV).

The wonder and charm of the grace of God is that this God is revealed to us in the Person of Christ. Paul's great ambition was to know the Lord Jesus and the power of resurrection. I trust that each one of us is seeking to do the same thing — to know Christ. Paul even renounced everything for this knowledge of Him. We also should seek to read and understand the Scriptures, for only then, as empowered of the Spirit, will we know Him in whom we have believed.

ק

19. QOPH – verses 145-152

David M Hughes

> "I cry out with my whole heart; Hear me, O
> Lord! I will keep Your statutes. I cry out to
> You; Save me, and I will keep Your
> testimonies. I rise before the dawning of
> the morning, and cry for help; I hope in
> Your word. My eyes are awake through the
> night watches, that I may meditate on Your
> word. Hear my voice according to Your
> lovingkindness; O Lord, revive me
> according to Your justice. They draw near
> who follow after wickedness; they are far
> from Your law. You are near, O Lord, and
> all Your commandments are truth.
> Concerning Your testimonies, I have known
> of old that You have founded them forever."

Introduction

One of my favourite things to do with my children is read
with them at bedtime. Sometimes we read storybooks.
Sometimes we read fact books about dangerous animals

or dinosaurs or cars. But my favourite books I read with them are stories that have been written as poems. I am not really sure what it is about them that I like. I think it is something to do with the clever use of words and the way the rhymes can be used to make ordinary sentences sound funny. I find poems and song lyrics strange things. I studied mathematics at University and now work in statistics, so it is safe to say that my brain works in a certain way. I like structure and logic and precise argument. But poems and song lyrics do not always have that. They make sense as a whole, at least usually, but you cannot analyse each line the way you can with some mathematical equation. And yet, even to my mathematical brain, poems and song-lyrics resonate with me. I think this is probably true of most people, whatever their natural gifting. There is just something about songs and poems that make them a good way to make a point, even when the argument is not as tight and precise as you might find in other parts of life.

The Psalms in the Bible are a good example of this. Many parts of the Psalms are so memorable. For example, many Christians know some of Psalm 23:

> "The LORD is my shepherd; I shall not want" (verse 1, KJV).

Even if we cannot recall all the words of any particular psalm, I think many Christians have found the Psalms to be a great source of comfort, encouragement and joy over many years, throughout Christian history. But if you have read any of the psalms, you will know that they are not meant to be read the same way you might read some of the apostle Paul's writings for example. The book of Psalms is certainly different to the book of Romans. But

God saw fit to include both in the Bible, because both have important messages for us to learn.

Prayer is Crying Out

Psalm 119:145-152 focus our attention on the link between the Word of God and prayer. So although the title for this book is *The Importance of God's Word*, prayer is the focus of this stanza. It shows how prayers are linked to the Scriptures. I have noticed themes, or ideas, which are developed about prayer in different ways in these eight verses. I will highlight a few of these ideas. Verse 145 starts with the words "I cry out" and I would suggest that the whole stanza details the Psalmist's "crying out" to God in three ways:

1. What we cry out.

2. How we cry out.

3. Who we cry to.

WHAT TO CRY OUT

What the psalmist cries out is important because it points to the kind of things we should be praying for. The first thing the psalmist cries out in verse 145:

> "Hear me, O LORD."

The psalmist wanted to be heard. He was not simply fulfilling a religious routine. This was not just a few words to recite diligently at the start or end of each day with little or no thought going into it. No, the psalmist prayed; in fact, he cried out, with his whole heart because he wanted the Lord to hear him. I wonder if I always pray like that? When I pray, how often am I consciously aware of the fact that I want the Lord to hear me.

There is a lovely description of God in Psalm 65 verse 2, where David says:

"O You who hear prayer."

That is a good verse to keep in mind when we pray. If we, like the psalmist in Psalm 119:145 cry out, "Hear me", we can have confidence (like David) that our prayer will be heard because God is the 'God who hears prayer'. There is just a cautionary note to be made here too:

"If I regard iniquity in my heart, the LORD will not hear" (Psalm 66:18).

Of course, it is not that God cannot physically hear my prayers if I pray whilst I am wilfully sinning and dwelling on sin in my heart. It is that God sees through my sham prayers whilst I have no intention of stopping the sins I am enjoying.

When it comes to the crying out of Psalm 119:145, the psalmist cries out with all his heart for the Lord to hear him. That is not the kind of heart that is dwelling on wrong things. That is the cry of a person who can be confident that the Lord will hear them. So when we pray, let us remember that God really does hear our prayers. Let us be conscious of that, and let it influence our conversation with Him.

After the psalmist cries, "Hear me" (verse 145), he cries, "Save me" (verse 146). Perhaps his prayer comes in a time of difficulty. The psalmist needed saving from some situation. Whatever trial we may find ourselves in, it is good that we can cry out to God to save us.

In verse 147, the psalmist has risen early in the morning to "cry for help." We might paraphrase this and say that the psalmist is crying "Help me." Perhaps there might be circumstances where the Lord does not remove the difficulties we face. The cry "Save me" is only partially answered. But the psalmist still cries "Help me." That was the lesson Paul had to learn:

> "And lest I should be exalted above measure by the abundance of the revelations, a thorn in the flesh was given to me, a messenger of Satan to buffet me, lest I be exalted above measure. Concerning this thing I pleaded with the Lord three times that it might depart from me. And He said to me, 'My grace is sufficient for you, for My strength is made perfect in weakness'" (2 Corinthians 12:7-9).

Paul had some kind of health issue, a "thorn in the flesh." To borrow the language of Psalm 119:146, he cried out to God, "Save me." He wanted to be delivered from whatever this problem was. But God had a plan for Paul that did not involve the removal of the problem. Instead, Paul had to learn that God's grace was sufficient for him. To borrow Psalm 119:146 words again, Paul had to learn to cry "Help me." There is a good lesson for us there. We each need to learn to rely on God's help, or His grace, each day in whatever trials we face. Let us cry out to God, "Save me," like the psalmist. It is natural, and surely right to ask God for deliverance from trials and difficulties. But let us also cry out to God, "Help me", and learn to trust God to help us by providing fresh grace to help us in each time of need, whether the trial is removed or not.

The final thing the psalmist cries out is "Revive me" (verse 149). That is another good thing for us to pray. In all the routines of life, the good and the bad, it is easy to lose energy and become tired. The psalmist's cry is a reminder not to try and struggle on in our own strength in such circumstances. We can cry out to God and ask Him to revive us and to give us fresh energy, fresh joy in salvation, and fresh perspective on each of today's challenges. I wonder if I am as quick as I should be to ask for this reviving from the Lord. Perhaps I miss out by looking for revival of my spirit in the wrong places! I am sure you could find all sorts of tips on the Internet for recharging your batteries. No doubt we have all tried plenty of them over the years. But surely my first response should be to cry out to God, "Revive me."

HOW TO CRY OUT

I have picked out some things that we can cry out to God: "Hear me," "Save me," "Help me" and "Revive me" – good things for us to model our own prayers on. Let us think now about how the psalmist cries out.

First, the psalmist said:

> "I cry out with my whole heart" (verse 145).

This was not a half-hearted prayer. He did not just ask God for help as a sort of last ditch "let's try anything" approach, in the way we might pass our *curriculum vitae* to anyone and everyone when we are job hunting. This prayer came out of a wholehearted dedication to God. Are our prayers like that?

Second, the psalmist's prayer was a responsive prayer:

- "I will keep your statutes" (verse 145).
- "I will keep your testimonies" (verse 146).

I do not think the psalmist is trying to bribe God here. He is not saying something along the lines of, "Dear God, please answer my prayer and then I will do everything you say" – in the way a child might say, "Please daddy let me have this toy. I will be really good, I promise." God is not bribed in such ways. Instead I think the psalmist is saying that he is prepared to act on whatever God reveals to him from God's Word (His statutes or testimonies). The psalmist prays, desperate that God would hear him and save him, and ready to put into practice in his life whatever God reveals to him. That's a good attitude to have. As you pray, asking God for guidance or help, are you willing to put into practice whatever challenges God shows you in His Word?

The psalmist's cry was a diligent cry:

- "I rise before the dawning of the morning and cry for help" (verse 147).

- "My eyes are awake through the night watches that I may meditate on Your word" (verse 148).

The point here is that the psalmist has this constant focus on God throughout the day. Both in the early morning and late evening, the psalmist is thinking about God and praying to Him. Perhaps this re-emphasises the point made earlier that prayer is not just an obligation to tick off a list every now and again, but a resource to be used frequently throughout the day. The psalmist kept on communicating with God. Day and night. Do I show a similar diligence in my prayers? Do you?

The psalmist's cry was a hope-filled cry:

"I hope in Your word" (verse 147).

The psalmist had confidence that God would hear his prayer because he read the Scriptures and believed what he read. What the psalmist read in God's Word gave him confidence in God. Are my prayers filled with similar hope and trust in God's Word?

The psalmist's cry was a thoughtful cry. The purpose of the psalmist being awake through the night watches is:

> "That I may meditate on Your word" (verse 148).

This is the key link between these thoughts on prayer and the rest of Psalm 119, which is all about God's Word.

The psalmist's prayers were biblical prayers. He thought about what he read in the Scriptures and he prayed accordingly. You can tell that the psalmist has a high view of God's Word by noticing the words he uses to describe it. He calls it:

1. "Your statutes" (verse 145).

2. "Your testimonies" (verses 146 and 152).

3. "Your word" (verses 147 and 148).

4. "Your law" (verse 150).

5. "Your commandments" (verse 151).

The psalmist views God's Word as precious because it is *God's* Word – that is the emphasised by his repeating of the word "Your". God's Word could be trusted and taken seriously, precisely because it was *God's* Word. And so the psalmist could confidently think about what he read and pray about it:

- He could pray that his life would reflect the moral conduct he read about.

- He could ask for help confident that God was certainly able to provide it.

- He could ask for reviving fully assured that God had ample resources to refresh and revitalise him.

The psalmist's meditation on the Scriptures informed his prayers. That would be an excellent habit for us to develop too. We should each read the Bible as often as we can. As we do so, are we growing in confidence in the God it reveals to us? Are we learning more about how we ought to pray? And do we pray about the things we read about?

TO WHOM TO CRY OUT

After what the psalmist cries, and how he cries, this stanza tells us about the God to whom the psalmist prays. First:

> "Hear my voice according to Your lovingkindness" (verse 149).

What an encouragement to the psalmist. He was not praying to a powerful despot who needed to be sweettalked in order to hear the petition. Instead he was praying to the God characterised by "lovingkindness." When we pray, we should remember that we pray to the God who is filled with lovingkindness. That is an encouragement to us to keep on praying!

Verses 150-152 are interesting because they describe the relationship of two groups of people to God. To those who are characterised by wickedness, and not following or obeying God's Word, God appears far from them:

> "They draw near who follow after wickedness; They are far from Your law" (verse 150).

These people may be coming near to the psalmist and causing him difficulties, but they are far from God. They do not know God's help and encouragement. They do not know Him as full of lovingkindness. They are far from Him. But contrast that with the next words of the psalmist:

> "You are near, O LORD, and all Your commandments are truth" (verse 151).

The psalmist had a sense of the nearness of the Lord. Even in difficulties he had the encouragement of the Lord being near to him. It is like David who says:

> "I will fear no evil for You are with me" (Psalm 23:4).

We should be those people who know the Lord's nearness, which will sustain us in whatever challenges we face. What an encouragement to pray! The psalmist was not crying out to someone distant, as if his prayers did not get higher than the ceiling of whatever room he was in. Instead, he prayed to the Someone he knew was near to him.

Conclusion

In this stanza of Psalm 119, there is a crucial link between the Word of God and our prayers. Our prayers should be biblical prayers. Let us always pray prayers which are informed by what we read in the Bible. Verses 146-152 inform us about the kind of things we should pray for and challenges us as to whether we pray in a similar way:

- They have described how we should pray. Do we show similar diligence in prayer and willingness to put into practice whatever God reveals to us?

- They have reminded us about the lovingly kind God to whom we pray and who is near to His people.

May the Lord help us to keep on treasuring His Word, and letting it influence our prayers!

ר

20. RESH – verses 153-160

Jonathan Hughes

Introduction

I remember when one of my sons was young, he found Egyptian hieroglyphics fascinating. Perhaps it was the idea that each symbol had a meaning as well as a sound, whereas the English alphabet is comprised of letters which only have a sound. Of course, it is not only the Egyptian alphabet that has this characteristic. Many of the Middle Eastern forms of writing have a similar property. In Hebrew, each letter of the alphabet has a meaning as well as a sound. For RESH, the twentieth letter of the Hebrew alphabet, that meaning is poor, or evil, or a bowed head (in much the same sense as we would speak about hanging one's head in shame).

> "The Talmud states: 'There is no poor person except he who is poor in knowledge' (Nedarim 41a). The *resh* is far away from God. He entertains flagrant, evil thoughts and speaks negatively. He is beyond the level of having or not having

money. He is *spiritually* bereft; the poorest
of the poor."[25]

The title of this book about Psalm 119 is *The Importance of
God's Word*. This stanza continues this theme and presents
the serious consequences when His Word is ignored. The
individual who knows and lives God's Word is rich,
whereas the individual who ignores God's Word is poor.
Another point to note is that three times within this
stanza the Psalmist prays that God will revive him. The
dictionary gives four possible shades of meaning to this
word revive:

1. It can mean to restore life or consciousness.
2. It may imply to give new strength or energy to
   someone or something.
3. It can mean to restore interest in or the popularity
   of something.
4. It can suggest improving the condition of
   something.

It would be a marvellous thing if, as we look at verses
153-160, God would revive us and our interest in His
Word. Perhaps you are feeling spiritually tired. Life is hard
sometimes and disappointments can mean that we lose
our joy and freshness and that just getting through a day
without giving up is about as good as we can manage.
Perhaps you have been so busy serving the Lord with no
obvious sign of benefit and you are just worn out with the
struggle. May He revive each one of us so that we can
face the future with a wholehearted desire to serve Him
faithfully in whatever circumstances we may face. So, we
will consider this stanza under the three prayers for
revival.

[25] Rabbi Aaron L. Raskin,
https://www.chabad.org/library/article_cdo/aid/137092/jewish/Resh.htm

Prayer I

"Consider my affliction and deliver me, for I do not forget Your law. Plead my cause and redeem me; revive me according to Your word" (verses 153-154).

Please read 1 Kings chapter 19. It is the story of Elijah in the immediate aftermath of his confrontation with the prophets of Baal on Mount Carmel. Elijah fled from the presence of King Ahab and escaped to the wilderness. There he rested in the shadow of a tree, wanting to die. He was met by an angel who provided food for him to sustain him in his journey. Elijah made his way for forty days and nights until he came to a cave on Mount Horeb. There he was to meet with God Himself. God asked him what he was doing there, to which Elijah answered that he had been so busy for God and he was so alone. Three powerful events shake Elijah's world, but God was not in any of them. Finally, he heard the voice of God speaking to him in a still small voice. That voice told him that God still had work for Elijah to do. It also told him of the many other servants that God had. Elijah's loneliness was perceived not real.

Verses 153-154, which are beautifully illustrated in the experience of Elijah, are a real word to any servants of the Lord who are feeling downcast and defeated. It is exciting and uplifting when we set out to serve God. When we see God at work, perhaps in the salvation of others, or by numerical growth or interest in what we are doing, we are sustained and encouraged. However, more often than not, in His service there are times when nothing seems to happen, and it becomes monotonous and hard work. We may begin to question our calling, our

231

suitability, and our sacrifice. Is it worth it? We may feel just as Elijah did that we serve alone and that it is all too much for us.

We can rest in the sure knowledge that He *does* consider us and will provide for us the strength for each day. It is such a lovely touch that before recommissioning Elijah, God feeds him physically. We too may need to rest physically before God has further work for us to do. And God will not only consider us but also deliver us. I doubt that Elijah would ever have thought in those dark moments on Mount Horeb that later in life he would be caught up to heaven, without dying, in a chariot of fire. Do we remember in our darker moments that we are waiting for that glorious call to meet with the Lord in the air? Our eventual success and glorification are assured, and this must sustain us through times of trouble.

The Psalmist would make remembering God's law a central part of his life and it is the basis upon which he prayed for revival in this stanza. It was not in mighty acts of power that Elijah heard the voice of God but in a still small voice. When we feel down and defeated, it is absolutely imperative that we make time for Bible reading and study. It is vital that we saturate our minds with His Word, to allow Him to speak to us. Read your favourite chapters or listen to His Word being read if you are too tired to read for yourself, but let His voice speak to you from the words of Scripture. Perhaps my favourite poem is entitled *The Pilgrim* by Henry N. Cobb, which recounts a conversation between a weary pilgrim and his heavenly Father.

Part of the conversation is:

> "The way is long, my Father! And my soul
> longs for the rest and the quiet of the goal;
> while yet I journey through this weary land,
> keep me from wandering. Father, take my hand,
> quickly and straight
> lead to Heaven's gate,
> Thy child!"

Then God answers the pilgrim:

> "The way is long, My child! But it shall be
> not one step longer than is best for thee;
> and thou shalt know, at last, when thou shalt stand
> safe at the goal, how I did take thy hand,
> and quick and straight
> lead to Heaven's gate,
> My child."[26]

Let us remember that it will never be one step longer than is best for us. God had further work for Elijah, as He may well have for us. His Word is sufficient to feed our souls and sustain us as we live in this world. May we never forget that!

Prayer 2

"Salvation is far from the wicked, for they do not seek Your statutes. Great are Your tender mercies, O LORD; revive me according to Your judgements" (verses 155-156).

They say that a picture paints a thousand words. I think that there is a beautiful episode in the life of the Lord Jesus that illustrates the Psalmist's second prayer for revival. In John chapter 8, we read about the time when

[26] In *The Changed Cross and Other Religious Poems*, Anson D. F. Randolph & Co: New York, 1872, page 128.

the scribes and Pharisees brought to Jesus a woman who had been caught in the very act of adultery. Outwardly, they wanted to stone her but what they really desired was to trip Jesus up and undermine His authority. So they asked Him what should be done. Undoubtedly, the law stated that the punishment for adultery was death.

What a terrifying scene this must have been. How frightened the woman must have been, the men's hatred palpable. Salvation was indeed far from these wicked men. They had no interest in the righteous observance of the law. They certainly had no interest in the woman – she was a mere object upon which they hatched their plot. Whilst outwardly seeking to uphold the law, their hearts were filled with hatred and their actions did not confirm that they were moved by a love for God. Their actions spoke of self-interest rather than a desire to honour God.

We live in a world that has not changed from those days. Mankind is still motivated by self-interest and hatred – hatred of those who have more than we do, hatred of the foreigner, hatred of the ones who are different. We say that we have right and just laws, but we have no interest in obeying God and being motivated by His desires. The fact that these scribes and Pharisees did not seek God's statutes is laid bare by the fact that the man involved was not brought to Jesus. If she had been caught in the very act, where was he? The devil knows that he will miss out on the glories of an eternity in the presence of God. In his malign vindictiveness, he now seeks those who will suffer alongside him. These scribes and Pharisees, dressed up in the robes of religious rectitude, were his willing prey and could not have been further from being saved. But the Psalmist then goes on to say:

"Great are Your tender mercies, O LORD"
(verse 156a).

Jesus bent down and started to write something in the ground. The scribes and Pharisees continued to press Jesus for an answer, to which He challenged them:

> "Let him who is without sin... cast the
> first stone" (John 8:7, paraphrased)

Again, He bent down and wrote in the ground. Did Jesus write their names in the dust and perhaps start to write down some of their sins? (see also Jeremiah 17:13). Who could stand such scrutiny? So they left, from the oldest first to the youngest until the woman was left alone with Jesus. He questioned her as to where her accusers were before telling her:

> "Neither do I condemn you; go and sin
> no more" (John 8:11).

That judgement of Jesus, so full of tender mercy, must have had the most profound effect on the woman. Whilst we do not read any more of her, so far as we know, I am sure that her life was radically different as a result of her encounter with Jesus. I am sure that she would have had a very clear recollection of those words whenever she was tempted to stray from marital faithfulness. She who had been a dead woman walking in life, had life restored to her and her condition was much improved. Revival always starts in the heart of the individual!

Perhaps there are things in your life that are not right. We can be assured that as we draw close to the Lord Jesus, we can find reviving strength. Through His Word, He will often speak to us and challenge us to be more like Him. The words, "Go and sin no more", could not have placed a heavier demand upon the woman. But in meeting Jesus she had met the One who was able to strengthen her so that she could find freedom in obedience. The Lord will never ask us to do something for Him for which He does not also empower us. This woman needed, and we need, to learn that true freedom is not found in being able to do whatever we like. It is found in willing obedience to Him.

Prayer 3

> "Many are my persecutors and my enemies, yet I do not turn from Your testimonies. I see the treacherous and am disgusted, because they do not keep Your word. Consider how I love Your precepts; revive me O LORD, according to Your lovingkindness" (verses 157-159).

Life can be tough sometimes. You try to do the right thing and seem to be very alone in doing that. I recognise that I am not a very patient person and sometimes I do try to be more so. It is just that whenever I do, everything and everyone conspires against me trying to slow things down and make things difficult. It is all too much! At other times, you read newspapers and think how anyone could ever think that what they were doing was right. How has humanity sunk to such a level that shocking events now seem routine and have lost the power to surprise! Perhaps this was how the Psalmist was feeling as he prayed for God to revive him. The events of life had left him feeling grubby and he was heart sick of the sin around him.

At the so-called Last Supper, Jesus took a towel and started to wash the disciples' feet. When Jesus came to Peter, Peter objected, until Jesus explained that Peter could have no part with Jesus unless he was washed. Peter exclaimed:

> "Then wash me all over" (John 13:9, paraphrased).

Jesus explained that it was just his feet that needed to be washed. As those who are saved, we have been washed all over, but as we live in this world, we are exposed to so many influences that leave us feeling dirty and impure. We very much need the washing of His Word for our daily living. We ought never to lose the sense of the wrongness of sin – the actions of the sinful should disgust us (but we must always love the sinner, as He does) and we need that daily cleaning effect of daily Bible study and prayer.

After a hot and dusty day's walking, how refreshing it would have been for those feet to be immersed in cool water and gently rubbed dry! As we are exposed to the materialistic influences of our society, the selfishness of the me-first attitude, we are going to become ground down and grubby. It is all too easy to start to adopt the standards of those around. Little by little, the dirt builds up and before long we have changed. The Psalmist was aware that those who rejected God were many, but he would not turn from what God had said. We will win no popularity contests as we seek to live out a biblical Christianity. That should not alarm us, nor should it deflect us from doing what is right.

Just the other day, my wife and I were shopping. She had bought our granddaughter a colouring book amongst other items and as we left the checkout, she realised that she had not been charged for it. So back we went, queueing up again to pay – yes, it was one of those lessons in patience days. The shop assistant gave her the strangest look as if she could hardly believe that someone was that honest! It was the right thing to do – but sadly illustrates how far society has fallen from doing what is right. So, the Psalmist had three times prayed for God to revive him. That leaves me with a challenge as to how much I long for the life-restoring, condition-improving revival of God.

Summary

"The entirety of Your word is truth, and every one of Your righteous judgments endures forever" (verse 160).

This may appear as a fairly innocuous statement to finish off this stanza with, but it is not! When was the last time you listened to someone telling you the truth, the whole truth and nothing but the truth? We are so used to hearing part-truths, truth with a personal gloss put on it, or evasive versions of truth that do not ring true. As you listen to politicians, as you listen to business people, as you listen to journalists, you are fed a diet of what is at best something like the truth and often far worse. Yet here the Psalmist is telling us, without a shade of doubt or barefaced audacity, that the entirety of God's Word is truth. Not just that every single verse is true but that when it is put together as a whole, it presents a perfectly true picture. God does not paint a picture of Himself that in any way distorts the truth. Nor does He speak of mankind in anything other than the truth. So, when He calls Himself the Creator God that is exactly what He is. When Jesus speaks of Himself as fully God, that is who He is. His Word stands as an absolutely true plumb line against which everything else must be judged. Nor will God act in a way that is not entirely consistent with His

Word. It is not that His Word says that we are sinners – which is true, and He is holy, which is also true, but that at the end of the day, He will just overlook all that because He loves us. No! Every one of His righteous judgements endures forever. Abraham knew this to be true of God when he declared:

> "Shall not the righteous Judge of all the
> earth do right?" (Genesis 18:25).

There are many events in life about which we just do not understand why. There are things in the Bible that we do not understand as to how they can be. That is because, with our finite minds, we are trying to understand the infinite. However, we can be fully sure that whenever God does something, He is acting in a way that is perfectly right. It is impossible for Him to do otherwise.

In an ever-changing world, when sometimes from one day to the next we do not know what is going to happen or how a matter is going to end, we can find a bedrock of certainty – that His Word and His judgments are eternal. As I commit myself to Him now, it is a commitment that will last the full length of eternity. There is no risk that He may grow tired of me and change His mind about my deserving a home in Heaven. That promise to make me one of His children is one that will stand the test both of time and eternity. No wonder that our God is unique. No wonder He is a God unlike any other. No wonder He deserves my praise, thanks, and worship, both now and in eternity!

שׁ

21.   SHIN – verses 161-168

David G Pulman

Introduction

SHIN has the meaning of tooth or teeth with both negative and positive connotations:

- The negative is seen in verses 161 and 163; the writer being persecuted by others and he hates those who are liars. These are the negative and destructive aspects of this stanza, which can be easily identified with the meaning of SHIN as teeth.

- The remainder of the stanza is positive, in which we may consider the meaning of SHIN (teeth) as tenaciously holding onto that which is positive.

Verse 161: "Princes persecute me without a cause, but my heart stands in awe of Your word."

In every dispensation the godly are persecuted by the ungodly. Lying is a characteristic of those who are controlled by Satan. He is the father of lies. It is one of the facts of life for a believer, that persecution can occur at any time and for no other reason than that they are a believer in the one true God and His Son Jesus Christ. In John 15:18-21, the Lord Jesus Christ warned that His followers would have persecution in the world. Therefore, let us not be surprised when trouble comes our way for no other reason than that we belong to Christ, our Saviour and Lord. On the other hand, the psalmist has confidence in such situations.

If rulers, that is the princes, persecute without a cause he has a 'but':

> "But my heart stands in awe of Your word" (verse 161b).

The psalmist is focused upon God's Word. His inner being – his heart, the place of affection – has due reverence for the Scriptures. In Hebrews 4:12, we are told that the Word of God is living and powerful. Time and again God's Word gives guidance for every circumstance, assesses situations to the minutest detail and pinpoints exactly what is required in any situation. This should guide us as to how we react to the persecution.

Verse 163: "I hate and abhor lying, but I love Your law."

The second negative of this stanza (verse 163a) is an almost universal characteristic of unbelievers, that of lying. Lying can often be a means of self-gain or avoiding responsibilities. In John 8:44, the Lord Jesus declares that the source of lying is Satan, the father of it. If we listen to Satan, as Adam and Eve did, we will reject God's Word and this will lead to rejecting God's principles, which were given to govern behaviour – how we live and interact with other people. As Christians, we are required to be open and truthful – not just with other Christians but with everyone.

Again, the psalmist has the positive answer. He cleaves to God's Word and desires to live by what he reads in the Scriptures:

"I love your law" (verse 163b).

Verse 162: "I rejoice at Your word as one who finds great treasure."

God's Word brings joy to the psalmist's heart. He rejoices and he finds treasure in the Scriptures. This treasure is likened to the spoils of war when victory has been achieved by a conquering army. You may think this is a strange consideration but let us consider that if we are to gain any real appreciation of God's Word, then it will take effort. It will cost us time and energy to study the Scriptures. Consider Psalm 45, which speaks of God's King. The psalmist came to these conclusions because he was occupied with his God and the Scriptures:

> "My heart is overflowing with a good theme; I recite my composition concerning the King; my tongue is the pen of a ready writer. You are fairer than the sons of men; grace is poured upon Your lips; therefore, God has blessed You forever" (Psalm 45:1-2).

Verse 164: "Seven times a day I praise You because of Your righteous judgments."

The writer of the Psalm praises God seven times per day. The use of number seven is interesting. Seven is a prime or cardinal number. It reminds us of the seven days in a week, six days of creation plus the seventh, when God rested from His work. We might then say that the writer of the psalm had a perfect appreciation that praise belongs to God. He praises because he understands that God's ways and decisions are right:

> "Because of Your righteous judgments"
> (verse 164b).

We also see that this is a daily activity to give praise to God. It should not be confined to a Sunday! This is a challenge to all Christians. Do we have things about which we can give praise every day? Are we thankful daily? One reason the psalmist had cause to praise was God's righteous judgments.

Sometimes we might read the Scriptures and find things are difficult to understand and not in line with current social, moral, and political thinking. The challenge to us, as it was to the psalmist, is to fall in line with God's Word, no matter how different and possibly unpopular it might be with the trends of the world. The world judges itself by its own and changing standards but we must judge ourselves by God's standards. The unbelieving world is moving towards condemnation, whereas believers are moving towards the eternal scene of the Father's house (see John 14:1-6).

Verse 165: "Great peace have those who love Your law, and nothing causes them to stumble."

Great peace may be considered as great safety. Safety is found in the Word of God. God's Word guides through the paths of life:

> "Your word is a lamp to my feet and a
> light to my path" (verse 105).

A lamp to the feet and a light to the path – to prevent stumbling, tripping, and falling.

Verse 166: "LORD, I hope for Your salvation, and I do Your commandments."

The psalmist hopes or waits for the salvation, or deliverance, that can only be fully realised by his God, Jehovah. Part of that deliverance is due to the writer heeding the warnings, the commandments not to do or follow specifically forbidden situations. The Garden of Eden is where we find the first of these commandments – Adam was told not eat of the tree of the knowledge of good and evil (see Genesis 2:17). But his disobedience led to disaster as far as mankind was and is concerned. Every wise prohibition in God's Word when disobeyed has brought about disaster in some measure. The world ignores God to its peril and Christians when failing to follow God's Word find themselves in difficulty.

Verse 167: "My soul keeps Your testimonies, and I love them exceedingly."

God's Word is not only "Do's and 'Do not's", but it also gives us a revelation of Himself. God is Holy and God is Love. An appreciation of this and the many other attributes of His divine nature are to instruct the believer; and they help us to understand why God teaches through His Word. The purpose is to conform us to His marvellous ways of blessing so that we see the importance of loving the Scriptures.

Verse 168: "I keep Your precepts and Your testimonies, for all my ways are before You."

In the last verse of this stanza, we are brought to the conclusion that God wants His people to know Him.

This verse ends with the psalmist realising that his God knows the future. For a safe and secure future, avoiding the unnecessary failures of life, we need to be conscious that:

> "All my ways are before You" (verse 168b).

Happy is the person who seeks to leave the future entirely in God's hands. How much more so, we in this dispensation, who know both the Lord Jesus Christ and God the Father and have a better relationship with them than the Old Testament saints ever had. We can leave our whole life in the hands of our loving Saviour!

ת

22.   TAU – verses 169-176

DAVID G PULMAN

Introduction

This last stanza of Psalm 119 is marked by the Hebrew letter TAU. TAU is said to represent the sign of a cross, although the letter when written does not look like a cross. TAU was seen on the coinage of the Maccabees, who succeeded for a time in giving the Jewish people national freedom, throwing off the rule and oppression of Antiochus Epiphanes. The cross speaks of suffering and in this last stanza the writer speaks about suffering and the need for help. The psalmist no doubt was relating to his own suffering and his distressing situations. Prophetically we can see that the stanza speaks to us of our Lord Jesus Christ. The end of His life in this world was by crucifixion.

Verse 169: "Let my cry come before You, O LORD; give me understanding according to Your word."

Again a common theme of Psalm 119 is taken up by the psalmist – the desire of the writer to know more, and to have a better understanding, of God's Word. His Word gives instruction for life – how to live right for God in this world. We can align this verse with Paul's instruction to Timothy:

> "Study to shew thyself approved unto God, a workman that needeth not to be ashamed, rightly dividing the word of truth" (2 Timothy 2:15, KJV).

Verse 170: "Let my supplication come before You; deliver me according to Your word."

The cry now becomes a plea, a supplication for God to be gracious, in order that the psalmist might be rescued from his situation. Whatever the psalmist's problem was (we are not told what), deliverance must be according to God's Word. The Lord Jesus in the Garden of Gethsemane said:

> "Father, if it is Your will, take this cup away from Me; nevertheless, not My will, but Yours, be done" (Luke 22:42).

As the Lord bowed to the will of His Father so we too need to submit to the Word of God – God's revealed will for us.

Verses 171-172: "My lips shall utter praise, for You teach me Your statutes. My tongue shall speak of Your word, for all Your commandments are righteousness."

As we have seen dependence upon God, we now see confidence in God. First, we have an outpouring of praise from the writer – no doubt thankfulness in his heart and confidence of a positive response from his

God. The writer of Psalm 111 has a similar burst of praise:

> "I will praise the LORD with my whole heart" (Psalm 111:1).

Praise in Psalm 119:171 is followed by an appreciation of God's Word, specifically statutes, or principles, that are always to be observed. The writer is thankful for godly instruction. Living according to God's Word gives daily guidance. It is a defence against evil; it delights the heart of God and gives assurance to the believer.

What was true in the psalmist's day is still true in our day. Praise is directed towards God, but we must also have a testimony towards our fellow man. This is expected from a Christian. So, like the psalmist, we ourselves must be ready to speak God's Word. People will only know what God expects from them by us making God's Word known to them – that salvation is only by accepting Christ as Saviour. In order to do this, they must recognise their total sinfulness and that they cannot earn a place in heaven and thereby escape God's righteous judgment. Salvation is totally and solely dependent upon the sacrifice of the Lord Jesus Christ and my acceptance of the fact that He died for me.

In the final part of verse 172, we find the psalmist recognising that he has a responsibility to follow God's instruction; it is a commandment that is enjoined upon him. If we proclaim God's Word, then we must support what we say by how we live. The righteousness of God's Word made it important for believers in the psalmist's day to live by the Scriptures. So, too, it is now important for those who say they are Christians, to live by the Scriptures.

Verse 173: "Let Your hand become my help, for I have chosen Your precepts."

The psalmist recognises his responsibilities because of his conscious decision to abide by God's precepts. But at the same time, he also recognises that to be effective in those responsibilities he needs God's assistance. As part of Adam's race, even though we know the Lord Jesus as our Saviour, we are still frail and far from capable in ourselves. It is good therefore to depend upon God to support and direct each one of us in living out the Christian life.

Verse 174: "I long for Your salvation, O LORD, and Your law is my delight."

The psalmist's longing has been an ongoing desire and it is focused upon Jehovah's salvation. We might simply view salvation as deliverance from an unwanted experience. However, salvation here also includes the thoughts of prosperity and victory. This may well have a more future application and as far as Christians are concerned, we can consider victory in more than one way. The Lord Jesus accomplished a victory as the One who gave His life and shouted with triumph:

"It is finished!" (John 19:30).

This was in connection with Him dealing with sin and dealing with a holy God's righteous demands as the Substitute for each person who accepts Jesus as their own personal Saviour. In addition, Christians wait the fulness of salvation at the Rapture event when all believers (both those who have died and those who are currently alive) will be caught up to meet the Lord Jesus in the air (see 1 Thessalonians 4:13-18). From that grand meeting, He will conduct us into His Father's house (see John 14:1-3).

When a Christian dies, their body is placed in a grave and it is considered to be asleep (1 Thessalonians 4:13-14). The spirit and soul, the non-physical parts of our being, go to be with Christ, which the apostle Paul describes as a condition which is far better (see 2 Corinthians 5:1-8 with Philippians 1:23). No doubt the psalmist has the same kind of considerations when he writes:

Verse 175: "Let my soul live, and it shall praise You; And let Your judgments help me."

The psalmist did not have the full understanding of God's purposes and ways and was unaware of the revelations that have been unfolded in the New Testament. So, when we consider the Old Testament from a Christian viewpoint, we do so with a measure of a fuller understanding of God's intentions. David wrote:

> "For in death there is no remembrance of You; in the grave who will give You thanks?" (Psalm 6:5).

Even David, who was close to the Lord, realised that death cut off the conscious ability to communicate praise. But the psalmist closes with the realisation that God always has the last word for every situation as he states:

> "Let Your judgments help me" (Psalm 119:175b).

God's decisions are final even though we desire that those decisions would be helpful to us in our lives. The psalmist is not looking for death but for a continuance of a life of praise. Christians look forward to a heavenly scene at the Rapture, when praise and worship will be taken up in those realms above.

Verse 176: "I have gone astray like a lost sheep; seek Your servant, for I do not forget Your commandments."

In the final verse of Psalm 119, the psalmist once again recognises the tendency to go astray. This verse reminds us of the parable of the lost sheep (see Luke 15:3-7), but we must also consider the Good Shepherd who gave His life for the sheep (see John 10:11). Without the sacrifice of the Lord Jesus there would be no salvation. As this psalm closes, we see that the writer does not forget God's commandments. The New Testament teaches us how we can be saved from the judgment, which is due to sinners. Salvation is only found in Jesus and in no other person or the rituals of any religion. The blessing of eternal life is a gift from Jesus the Son of God to those who accept Him as Saviour.

Conclusion

In this book, we have endeavoured to demonstrate *The Importance of God's Word*. Throughout this consideration of Psalm 119, we have highlighted the various words employed to describe the subtle meanings the psalmist used to describe the Word of God, for example, commandments, law, precepts and so forth. Additionally, we have seen the commitment expressed by the psalmist – his reliance upon his God and the necessity of seeking always the resource found in Jehovah his God. In parallel we have endeavoured to link the teaching of the psalm to our everyday experience as Christians.

The first stanza, with the Hebrew letter ALEPH, introduced the blessedness of the obedient servant. How well it described the perfect service of our Lord Jesus Christ!

The last stanza, with the Hebrew letter TAU, reminds us that for us, as for the Lord Jesus Himself, suffering finally leads to triumph.

www.ingramcontent.com/pod-product-compliance
Lightning Source LLC
Chambersburg PA
CBHW062049080426
42734CB00012B/2595